THE PEOPLE'S CHOICE

THE PEOPLE'S CHOICE

Philadelphia's William S. Vare

J. T. SALTER

An Exposition-University Book

EXPOSITION PRESS   **NEW YORK**

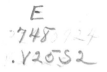

EXPOSITION PRESS INC.

50 Jericho Turnpike   Jericho, New York 11753

FIRST EDITION

LIBRARY OF CONGRESS CATALOG CARD NUMBER: 72-164867

0-682-47326-X

48728

For my wife,

KATHARINE SHEPARD HAYDEN SALTER,

whom I married in 1921,

the year that I was graduated from Oberlin College.

One of the happy things about Katharine

is that now, in 1971,

she is even dearer and more interesting

to live with than she was in 1921.

Of course this may be because she is a poet

and a historian, and a brilliant woman.

THE PEOPLE'S CHOICE

I

Never in the history of Republican politics had the leaders of all Philadelphia's wards been brought together under the will and guidance of one man until the organization which had been built and cemented together in the days of Thaddeus Stevens, irreconcilable foe of Abraham Lincoln, was inherited by William S. Vare. In 1922, when the powerful Ed Vare died, Bill Vare was not seriously regarded as an outstanding leader; he was just the younger brother in a great political family. Yet in a short time he revealed that he, too, was a man—the biggest of all the Vares. For he soon established a dictatorship stronger than that of any of the eight feudal barons who had ruled Philadelphia for eighty-four years before him—William B. Mann, Robert Mackey, James M'Manes, David Martin, Israel Durham, Boies Penrose, and Edwin H. Vare.

Outwardly Bill Vare differed from his brothers and the municipal bosses who had occupied the throne before him. And it is probable that he could never have achieved high place in politics without the start given him by his genial brothers, George and Ed. Given this boost, he consolidated and added to the position bequeathed to him. He first of all surrounded himself with a few of Ed Vare's friends, and then by contacts with key people and through the exercise of certain personality traits he became leader. Outstanding among these traits were his political astuteness, his unusual energy, his remarkable patience and determination, his unwillingness to surrender this side of death. He had also an exceptional memory, great resourcefulness, a marked capacity for details, and a record for truthtelling (i.e., man to man) that has not even been impaired by a cherry-tree story.

William S. Vare agreed with Machiavelli, of whom he never had heard, that if a prince cannot be both loved and feared, it is better to be feared. "He is a tough ringmaster," to put it in the words of one of the two most powerful ward leaders working with him. It was fear that held not only political leaders but all who realistically hoped or might grow to hope for preferment from the voters of Philadelphia.

It was this element of fear that handicapped me a hundred times in my effort to talk to the point with the men and women who knew Vare. Surprising as it may seem, his bitterest enemies (those that had broken from him, denounced him in the press, and tried to knife him when he lay critically ill) usually outdid the faithful in singing paeans of praise whenever his name was mentioned. Once at the home of an old Penrose lieutenant, and at the end of a two-hour conversation that had become more realistic as the talk progressed, I asked what might have been a searching question about Vare. The old ward leader started to answer, but he had barely finished one sentence before a shrill female voice from the second floor cried out, "George, please come here this minute!" When George returned, we talked about other matters.

Vare's friends will not talk. One of his closest advisers in 1933 explained it all to me when he said: "One story stands out in my memory. In those early campaigns we worked day and night and it was our custom to dine together in a nearby hotel. For three nights in succession I noticed a prominent man dining and each evening he escorted a different woman. On the third evening I remarked this to Mr. Vorhees, the campaign manager, and he looked at me calmly and said, 'I never saw that man here before.' 'Oh, you must have,' I replied eagerly. 'This is the third time he has been here, and each time he has had a different woman.' Again he answered, 'I never saw that man here before.' 'Why,' I insisted, 'I saw you speak to him.'

" 'Listen, youngster,' he said, 'you are very young and new in this game. In politics you never see or hear anything. Did you ever see that man here before?'

" 'No,' I replied carefully, 'I never saw that man here before.' "

This incident had occurred thirty years before, when the

storyteller was very young. All seasoned politicians, however, whether of yesterday or today, know the wisdom revealed here without being able to tell when it was first learned. It is part of them even as are their facial expressions and their clothes.

Vare was a better judge of issues than of men. The fact that he was the first influential person in Pennsylvania to take an unmistakable stand for repeal of the 18th Amendment shows that he had an eye for issues; yet one can only begin to understand why he placed certain men in high public office as his personal lieutenants when one accepts the idea that a minister's loyalty to the throne is of more value to the man on the throne than are his talents. (Loyalty may often be sufficient, provided the leader is well; but when he is weak and incapacitiated, more than loyalty is required—there is in some relationships no substitute for brains.) But even on the sole score of picking loyal men, Vare grievously erred on occasion, as the story of his life will show.

He was not at the head of his organization because of any unusual intellectual or social acumen. He was in no sense a cultured or highly civilized person. He had never had time to read, and he knew nothing of the liberal arts. He was ignorant and uninformed about many of the implications of the social process of which he was a part. But he was an ultraspecialist in ward and city politics. He was the politician without informed ideas on the majority of great public questions; but instead of a high order of intelligence, he possessed a "happy shrewdness" that enabled him to succeed where more intelligent men had failed. He saw with an eye single to the fifty wards in Philadelphia and the 1,566 divisions within these wards. With appropriate changes the following statement by Penrose to Talcott Williams would aptly fit Vare's philosophy of a lifetime:

> What's the use? I propose to stay senator. I want power. It is the only thing I crave. I have it. I shall keep it. There are about twenty-thousand to twenty-five thousand Republican workers who carry divisions and bring out the vote. I must know all these men. They must know me. If I do not meet them and never see them, I must know where they are, what they want, and how and when. My hand must always be on the job. I can never take it off; if I

do, I am gone. The interests of the state? Of course, I look after those. But the job is managing and knowing the twenty-thousand men who run the election divisions. As for great measures and issues, such as you talk about, no Senator of a state this size, run as it is, has the time to take them up. I am always glad to hear suggestions. Come to me, write to me. I shall always be glad to hear you, but staying senator is my job. ("After Penrose, What?" *The Century Magazine,* 105:49-55-N.22.)

In the pages that follow I shall attempt to describe Vare as he was. I write about him, not because he possessed any particular color, interest, magnetism, or political "it," but because he was the leader of the Philadelphia organization.

II

The story of William Scott Vare's life was one of which he could and did make large political capital. For the rise of the Vare family is a saga of America as epic in its proportions as is the history of the great economic barons of the nineteenth century. Where but in America could the Vare brothers have become powerful enough to rule a great city? The Vares were farm boys, rude, uncouth, but energetic and amazingly patient; they came out of the Neck (the low, mosquito-infested flatlands of muck, reeds, and ditches which skirt the Delaware, far down in South Philadelphia) to become the government which ran the government of Philadelphia, the inevitable human equation functioning in the urban democratic community.

Bill Vare was born on December 24, 1867, the youngest of ten children. His ancestry was English: his father came as a youth from the isle of Jersey in the English Channel; his mother, Abigail Stites, descended from Puritan stock. The father was a truck farmer who had picked out the swamps of South Philadelphia as holding possibilities for tillage. The Vare boys helped their father dig into the black, dripping soil, and helped to lay the foundation of the home that replaced the first structure. Bill lived the life of a farmer's son. But at the age of twelve, the year after his father was killed by a horse, he went to work as a cash boy in the Wanamaker store, at $1.50 a week, to help his widowed mother.

Vare's mother was a religious woman, whom Bishop Berry once characterized as a "faithful soul, plain, transparent, deeply spiritual, and with a perfect passion for Christian service." She was greatly beloved by all of her sons. Vare's father and elder brother (the one who died later from the bite of a hog) helped build a new Methodist Episcopal church for the people of his section; his father and three elder brothers supplied a team gratis and dug out the cellar. Vare himself was then a small boy in Sunday school and could not help in the construction. During his first term as recorder of deeds in Philadelphia, however, he gave his year's salary of $10,000 in order to lift the mortgage from this church, of which he said, "It is very dear to my heart." In recognition of Vare's helpfulness, the congregation renamed the church the Abigail Vare Methodist-Episcopal Church.

During the earlier years of his married life Senator Vare attended his mother's church. The man who was its pastor in those days told me that he greatly admired Senator Vare—that Vare would always give whatever help was asked for. On at least one occasion he gave $5,000 toward the payment for improvements in the church that were costing $10,000. "Much earlier, when the Vare boys were cleaning streets they would take the ashes out of the church and not charge a cent." When the Reverend Doctor X resigned his charge, Vare continued to contribute toward the salary of the new minister. But the new man got to talking about social and political matters; Vare withdrew his support, and the preacher was removed. When Vare was congressman he was able to get one of his constituents appointed as chaplain at Washington. This chaplain slipped in the congressional atmosphere— told risqué stories, etc.—and Congressman Vare had him removed too.

In 1930 the political leader sent for his spiritual adviser, the Reverend Doctor X, and said, "I have been thinking of my early life, Doctor, when we would come to your church. I would like to have you pray with me." And there, in the great living room of Vare's Atlantic City home, the two men prayed. Vare believed in God, and the Republican party. He wasn't given to discussing life after death or the nature of God. His clergyman added, "He was never bothered about questions of that sort. His religion was the religion of the church. He accepted all on faith. He was not the sort to ask questions about God. It was all a matter of faith with him. Penrose was quite different; he never thought of religion at all."

When Bill gave up his job in the Wanamaker store, three years later, he was receiving $2.50 a week. He tried one more year at school (Vare described himself to me as an average student there) and then joined his brother George in the produce business. Together the two boys induced their mother and brothers to invest in a horse and wagon; and they went through the streets selling vegetables. Thus as a boy he saw the public at first hand from his seat on a huckster's wagon. And he saw not only the people but also the needs of the growing district; so when he was in the City Council he could effectively serve his constituents.

"This experience," said Vare, "was to serve me in good stead in my later activities in politics; for it gave me an unusual personal acquaintance with the people of my native district of South Philadelphia and it gave me likewise a direct intimate knowledge of the needs of that section. Friends I made at that time remained my friends for many years to come, and I recall only recently a lady of my acquaintance reminding me that she was a customer on one of our routes more than forty years ago."

Bill Vare became a political worker before he was old enough to cast a vote. "My entry into active politics was a natural development. My brother, George, with whom I was engaged in business, had become one of the leaders among the younger Republicans of the first ward, and it was only natural that I likewise should become interested. I learned politics in the practical school of ringing doorbells and holding the checklist of voters on election day. Shortly after I reached my majority I was elected to the ward committee from my own division."

Living in the Neck, the edges of which were common dumping grounds, the Vare boys saw an opportunity to convert their political assets into cash. Ed Vare obtained a small city contract for the collection of ashes when he was twenty-one. The next year he was awarded a large municipal contract for street cleaning. It was profitable. They extended their operations, fought for and obtained more contracts, until finally they had a business employing hundreds of men, carts, drays, and much street-cleaning equipment. In ten years the brothers handled more than $13 million in city contracts. They reached out as general contractors for great constructions. Making millions, they turned their profits back with a free hand to increase their political power, which enabled them to make even more money. But as this vicious circle widened, and their wealth and power increased, the Vares never lost the common touch. For they knew that this was one of the qualities that enabled them to succeed. From the height of power Bill Vare could look back and analyze clearly the reason for his brother George's success in his fight in the first ward against the old Hog Combine. Vare pointed out:

> His [George's] very environment proved his greatest asset. He was in all truth to the manner born. He was not only a native of and raised in the first ward, then the "neck," but he was its living representative. A farmer's boy, a truck dealer, and a small contractor, he probably had met more men than any other man in the entire section. Easy of approach and always considerate of the feelings of others, he had made many warm friendships which were to serve him. Lacking resources, financial and otherwise, he gave generously of his time and energy.[1]

Once Penrose called William S. "the ash-cart stateman;" and this appellation was accepted for what it was worth in votes at the polls. Ed Vare once told a newspaperman, "We're not ashamed of our parents or our friends or the work we did on our way up in the world." Ed continued, "This is the district I worked when I was growing up. [They were standing on the corner of Ionic Street.] Many and many a morning before daylight I came out of this alley carrying half a barrel of swill on my shoulders. If Penrose and his crowd find anything to laugh at or sneer at in that, let them go ahead." None of the three brothers ever, for a

moment, lost this common touch; and it was one of the qualities
that enabled them to succeed.

When Bill Vare died, the Philadelphia *Bulletin* (had it fought
Vare?) recalled that "for years there was always a Christmas
party at the Alhambra or the Plaza theatres where thousands of
youngsters would be given toys and candy and a free show; and
Bill Vare would talk to them and tell them how proud he was
that he was born in South Philadelphia, that he had grown up
there as a poor boy, walking miles to work as he earned $1.50 a
week to help that family that had lost its chief breadwinner, the
father, when he was 11, and how the greatest things in life were
to remember the teachings of parents and the lessons studied in
school. Although never an orator, he was frequently called upon
to address Sunday School assemblies and church gatherings, where
he was wont to tell the story of his religious beliefs learned from
his devout mother."[2]

When he campaigned for his first city-wide office—recorder of
deeds—in 1901, his appearance on the platform was crude, and
so was his language. He was a huckster, and he looked the part.
"I remember him in that campaign. I was a young lawyer—had
just been admitted to the bar—and I had the natural feeling that
a young lawyer might have about that kind of person." (To quote
one who later held high public office in Philadelphia.) These
early campaigns made an impression on Vare too. He began to
study elocution and grammar at the Neff College of Oratory, for
the sake of the future; and he was also tutored by Francis Shunk
Brown, his candidate for governor in 1930. He improved, and
acquired a veneer that enabled him to stand up before a crowd
anywhere "without making a fool of himself." But speechmaking
was not his forte, and he never spoke with charm, distinction, or
eloquence. The speeches of the organization were given by the
Kellys and the Becks. The one significant thing about his public
speaking was his improvement—not the state that he had reached
but the distance he had come. In 1926—two years before he
suffered his stroke—I heard him deliver an address at the Elks
Hall, before four or five thousand party workers plus the ward
leaders of Philadelphia and many county leaders from the state.

There was thunderous applause as he strode onto the platform. He shook hands with different leaders as he approached the center of the stage. The fluent Harry Mackey, then his campaign manager in his fight for the Senate—later the first man who reached for his crown—eulogized him in an eloquent introduction. Then Vare spoke the approved, matter-of-fact statements that were spoken a thousand times in this expensive senatorial campaign. His voice was hard as stone; there was no fire, no enthusiasm; it was not a pleasant voice to hear, but everyone at the huge meeting heard it. He didn't unbend a single moment. He couldn't. He spoke his piece and sat down. Again everyone cheered—and the members of a ward committee know how to cheer!—and this night there were forty-eight committeemen present—a testimonial to the unity that a single leader had wrought in the organization. (Of course, he hadn't done it by making speeches!)

Because the Vares were *of* the people, the corollary that they were *for* the people was propounded by Vare's boosters. Vare was even compared to Lincoln in his humble start, his later success, and his championship of the "cause of the people." Senator Schall of Minnesota, a staunch supporter of Vare during the Vare fight to receive his seat in the Senate, blamed Vare's rejection by the Senate on "the nasty nice, who don't like to see the common people in power." In an outburst of praise, at the banquet given by Vare in 1931, Schall proclaimed; "Here Bill Vare stands for what the La Follettes stand for in Wisconsin. He is the friend of the plain man."[3] State Senator Salus, a loyal Vare man to the end, in discussing the Senate's refusal to seat his chief, gave it as his opinion that it was due to Vare's espousal of the "plain people" as against the "interests." And the recent revolution of our own organization," the Senator declared, "I believe was also due to his championing of the cause of the plain people as against the interests."

Vare himself made much of his active interest in the cause of "social legislation." Perhaps Vare realized, as Walter Lippmann has pointed out, that the number of people to whom any organization can be a successful valet is limited, and the far greater number of voters cannot be held by personal favors. For the anonymous multitude, therefore, Vare had ready the most telling propaganda that a politician could have prepared since the days of Roosevelt-Wilsonian progressivism.

Vare had some basis for claiming that he had been the people's champion fighting for legislation which would benefit them. Gifford Pinchot, his most bitter political enemy, admitted at the time of Vare's death: "In the past he and I have differed about many things. But we worked together heartily for old-age pensions and other social measures for the benefit of the people. These things I cannot forget."

> As I review my political career [Vare reminisced] I enjoy the keen satisfaction that the power which organized politics placed in my hands, and in those of my brother, was used in behalf of legislation which has been advantageous to the public of my own state and which was enacted against great opposition some years ago. . . . Political influence may be a power for good, and does not necessarily have to be utilized as a force for evil, as the demagogues so frequently charge in their efforts to gain control for themselves. . . . I have endeavored to use the organized machinery of the Republican party to serve the interests of the public and am satisfied that more lasting results have been secured through these definite constructive methods then would have been gained by following various chimerical reform or independent movements, usually led by so-called independents, more ambitious for personal aggrandizement than swayed by patriotic impulses.

Of course, this eulogy of machine politics cannot be taken entirely at face value, but it stands as a matter of record that the Vares supported and voted for the workmen's compensation laws, the child labor laws, the mothers' assistance bill, the act to regulate the hours of women in industry, and approval of the constitutional amendment extending the franchise to women. And it was the governor whom Vare forced upon Penrose—Brumbaugh—who forced through the 1915 legislature the workmen's compensation and child labor bills, the first of their kind in Pennsylvania.

From his more than forty years of observation Vare arrived at the conclusion that statesmen generally are those men who are willing to accept the highest positions in the government without being willing to work for them. As for himself, he was willing, he said, to stand on Webster's definition of a politician—"one versed or experienced in the science of government." He said that it was only common sense to believe that one trained in politics, as in any other field of endeavor, becomes an expert in this field and is therefore best qualified to handle great governmental affairs. Experience is a sine qua non in any profession, and this applies to politics. (One might add that it applies *especially* to politics, for the art of governing, as Lippmann says, happens to be one of the most difficult arts which men practice.)

As the Vares gained in political skill and power they wanted glory too, and it was through William that they hoped to get it. He was groomed to be not the politician of the family but the statesman. His brothers attempted to place him above and apart from the ward-leader type. To some of his friends and observers he looked like a statesman physically. His face was strong; it had a stubborn, almost adamant strength in it. His head was thrown back, and carried with an air of confidence and something of truculence; there was a confident surety about his whole bearing— that of the modest man who is nevertheless very certain of himself. His mouth was stubborn too, and rather thin-lipped; only rarely did it break into a smile. His chin was that of a man who always enforced his own will and never yielded to an obstacle. He was not a tall man—before his stroke he stood not more than five feet nine—but there was something in the set of his shoulders and poise of his head that made him seem taller, and unusually powerful, though he weighed only about 175 pounds.

In 1911 his brothers tried to make him mayor, but Penrose and McNichol bitterly and successfully fought the nomination. Penrose knew that he who is the cause of another's becoming powerful is ruined. Vare lost the primary to Penrose's man, Earle, but the independent, Rudolph Blankenburg, beat Earle in the election, and with Vare's help. Victory here would have helped establish Ed Vare's younger brother Bill as a statesman, as admission to the Union League Club would have done also. Vare's name was proposed for membership by a former governor, Edwin S. Stuart, one of its strongest members, but he was never accepted in this highbrow citadel of Republicanism.

Vare first cast his eyes upon the Senate in 1922 after Penrose had died suddenly. His brother Ed went to Governor Sproul and demanded that "our Will" be appointed. Sproul refused and named G. W. Pepper. Ed died. So did Sproul. The last of the Vare brothers bided his time and built up his power. Slowly but inevitably he gathered the reins of power in Philadelphia. In 1926 he struck.[4]

In 1926, after having served fourteen years in the lower house in Washington, Vare reached for the United States Senate. The Senate was the one thing nearest his heart. "I have seen upwards of fifty men go from the House to the Senate. I decided to run, although I knew what I was up against." At that time he was opposed by Governor Pinchot; the senior senator, George Wharton Pepper; the junior senator, Dave Reed; the powerful Mr. Grundy; the outstanding member of President Coolidge's cabinet, Mr. Mellon—a man reputed to possess the fifth largest bankroll in the United States; and last, and very important, a united press. Yet he defeated the entire sextet. He and his group won the nomination, and reported an expenditure of $785,934. Pepper lost, although his group put at least $1,804,979 into this great primary struggle. Three years later the United States Senate refused Vare admission, not for any illegal act, but for general reasons similar to those that closed the portals of the Union League to him: he was a ward politician without social background. Shortly after the Senate's verdict Vare had a stroke, due undoubtedly to the strain of the Senate's prolonged inquiry. It was his fate to be not a statesman but a politician.

III

Vare did not reach his high position because of a charming or appealing personality. He was cold, reserved, taciturn, self-contained, and remote.

Perhaps he believed that statesmen must act the part, and that only fools laugh in public. He seemed formal, conventional, and still. His close friends were few. The men to whom he was deeply attached could be counted on the fingers of two hands. All the rest of his associates were more or less impersonal—pieces on the political table to be dealt with as the master would move figures on a chessboard.[5] He was just the reverse of his big brothers, George and Ed, who were spontaneously and enthusiastically loved by most members of the party organization. Each had a rare genius for making friends; unlike Bill, they seldom thought of appearances or the niceties as such. Ed was rough and ready and did not stand on ceremony. One night the 39th Ward organization held a campaign meeting. The first speaker started to eulogize Ed Vare. "Stop that bullshit and talk about the campaign!" protested the straightforward Ed. I saw old-time politicians with tears in their eyes when they talked of Ed. "I love that man, Professor!" said a kindly-looking deputy in the sheriff's office, "Where would I be today if it hadn't been for Ed? I would be working down on the docks, that's where!"

But Bill Vare's capacity for drawing people to him was not of that sort. He had no social tact or natural conviviality, as the following ancedote reveals. In 1917 a state senator from one of the upstate mining districts met two of his constituents, rough diamonds from the mines, in Philadelphia. He took them through City Hall, visiting many offices, and finally said, "Well, I'll take you over and introduce you to the big boss [Ed Vare] in the Betz Building, South Penn Square." They went in to see Ed, who greeted them in his cordial manner. ("I've always thought Ed was an ace!") After talking to Ed, they started to leave; they had not thought of seeing Bill. However, Ed, who thought that his younger brother was a little wonder and entitled to everything that could be thrown his way, asked them, just as they were leaving, if they had seen the congressman. The upstate leader answered no. (He had not even thought of seeing Bill.) Ed said, "He is right over here in his office. Come on over!" They went over. The senator introduced his two constituents to William S. They shuffled about uneasily because they immediately felt a difference—they were less comfortable than they had been in the presence of Ed. After coughing a little, Bill said, "Sit down, gentle-men; make yourselves at home; I was a roughneck once myself." He lived in a grim world, not a genial or humorous one. He did not naturally see the gayer side of the struggle for dominion. (He was not, however, altogether beyond a little practical joking. Once when he was a member of the City Council, he was one of a committee that accompanied the Liberty Bell to the Chicago Ex-position. Another politician on this committee was big George Edwards, who, in addition to weighing more than 300 pounds, wore long, flowing whiskers. While sitting in a parlor car he fell asleep. Councilman Vare conceived the idea of getting some damp sugar and rubbing it through the flowing whiskers. A myriad of large flies discovered the sweetness before Councilman Edwards came to life; when he did, he responded violently, and swore that he would put this upstart political leader out of business!)

In attempting to explain the rise of this man to the leadership of the most efficient Republican party organization in any Ameri-can city, one finds a blending of factors of cumulative weight. The first one was undoubtedly this—that although W. S. Vare did not have an appealing or charming personality himself, both George and Ed did possess that great political asset to a marked degree. These older brothers had an unusual capacity for making friends, and they founded the Vare fortune, both in dollars and in votes. Bill Vare was never alone until Ed died in 1922; but from that time on he went ahead; and he ultimately reached heights never approached by either of the two more likable brothers.

Another reason for his power was that he had an almost in-credible capacity for remembering and considering details. He knew not only the ward leaders but the names of a majority of the 3,000 ward committeemen throughout the city. Most of them he could call by their first names; he could describe the setup of factional situations not only in the divisions of South Philadelphia (the original Vare stronghold) but in other districts too. "Let a ward leader go in from Germantown and tell Vare about the various sections, and he will find that Bill Vare knows pretty near as much about it as he does—Italians, colored people, or any-body." In the summer of 1931 Vare was sitting on his porch in

Atlantic City talking to an uptown leader who tried to impress upon the Senator what a difficult task he had with certain sections. Vare said, "I know that you have four divisions that are 90 per cent Italian." The organization was built on such human contacts; the sum of these contacts was the limit of Vare's power. It is the boss's business to know his ward committeemen —and this boss knew them. Colonel X was present at Midvale at a dinner in 1903; Congressman Vare was also at the dinner. Vare had secured pertinent data concerning every guest: "For example, he knew the name of my [Colonel X's] policeman, and he wanted to know if I knew him and if I had ever asked any favors of him!" To quote a close friend:

> He had a remarkable memory throughout his life. He would sit down and give you the details of a contest that took place twenty-five years ago. When he would be out with me on the boat he might be still for ten or fifteen minutes, then suddenly he would turn around and talk for an hour solid about a whole campaign and how it was handled and the people interested in it. And he talked two hours at a streak after the convention which nominated Hoover, and he would tell you the details of that convention. He would just give you the details of everything—private meetings and who tried to influence him, etc., I would say that he is very companionable with a few people. One night when we were out together two men out of the twelve did all the talking. You couldn't do any talking yourself—they'd get agoing, and no one could get an oar in. I've heard Vare talk for three hours at a straight-going—on politics, nothing but politics.

As another person put it—one who was not in the Vare camp—"He thoroughly believed in himself and would recount his own political achievements as long as he had an audience. This was an evidence of extreme egotism to those not interested. Probably his dependents thought it pleasant reminiscences." Vare completely adopted Napoleon's idea of warfare, "Beat them in detail," and the reason that he was able to do this was that he had these details ineradicably on his mind.

That Vare was a consummate strategist in political affairs goes without saying. He was a man who "knew what to do," and the best way to illustrate his political skills is to tell the story of some of his characteristic political moves.

One of the clearest demonstrations of his power and resourcefulness was the Shoyer sticker campaign—a campaign that was waged and nearly won in one day, the third of November, 1925. John M. Patterson, Republican nominee for district attorney, was seriously ill on election day. He had been operated on for gallstones a few days before. His increasingly serious condition had greatly worried Vare and the other leaders in Philadelphia. Vare received frequent reports on Patterson's condition, and when he was told that the candidate would die that day, he and the more important ward leaders conferred and decided to abandon Patterson and support a new man—Frederick J. Shoyer. At the conclusion of this meeting Vare issued a statement that he was grieved almost beyond expression at the turn for the worse which Judge Patterson had taken. "Doctors say that there is no hope." It was then twelve o'clock, and within half an hour organization workers were passing out stickers bearing the name of Shoyer instead of Patterson on the ballot. The leaders had taken the stickers to the polling places as quickly as possible, but it was not until three o'clock that some of the outlying wards got theirs. The polls were to be closed at 7 P.M. The organization had from four to six and a half hours in which to wage a campaign and elect a candidate. Workers were instructed to have voters paste the Shoyer stickers on the ballot. In certain wards, however, voters found the Shoyer sticker already on the ballot when they entered the booth. The inquiring voter was told that Patterson had died and that Shoyer was the organization candidate now. Whether the voter or the party committeeman pasted the sticker on the ballot depended on the neighborhood in which the voting was done. The vote for district attorney was:

> Patterson, Republican 167,526
> Shoyer, Sticker 123,616
> Brennan, Democrat 25,679

This was a unique demonstration of the remarkable strength and efficiency of Vare's organization. And if the leader had not been nodding a little, at that, he would have previously instructed all party workers to retard voting until later in the day. For, as he said to me, "The only reason that Shoyer was not elected at the time that Patterson was dying was because too many ballots had been put in beforehand."

This singular example of organization influence stands, regardless of the means employed to exert it. Its power to roll up more than 100,000 votes for a man whose candidacy was never announced until the middle of election day was demonstrated. A question may be raised concerning the legality but not the efficiency of the party technique.

The day following the election I talked to one of my student friends who had served as an election official. He said that the Shoyer vote would have been greater but that in his division the officials started filling in the total vote for the different candidates early in the day. "We would mark off 100 votes in the lines reaching across the page. When the word came to switch to Shoyer we did not know what to do, for we had already given nearly all the votes to Patterson. However, we put Shoyer's name directly underneath Patterson's; Patterson got the 100 votes on the first line and Shoyer got all the rest—100 for Patterson, 267 for Shoyer, 3 for Brennan." He explained why the votes were not counted: "A fellow would go crazy counting votes—he would have to stay at the polls until five o'clock in the morning! One thing that we did not do at that election was to vote phantoms. Of course, I put in a vote for my mother and sister, for I knew they would swear to it if any question arose."

(This is descriptive of voting in a controlled area; in other sections the votes were faithfully counted instead of estimated; the procedure followed in a given area depended on the mores of the inhabitants of that area. The interesting thing is that whether the votes were counted or whether they were estimated, the organization got them; and if it had had twenty-four hours more to wage Shoyer's campaign, it would have elected him, and it could have done this without stealing a single vote.)

Vare and the other leaders were bitterly criticized for having "knifed a friend as he lay dying." Senator Vare stated his position on this case in these words:

I had been having daily contacts with doctors. They thought that Patterson would live. I couldn't ask Patterson to resign. However, I had a duty to perform, an obligation that I owed the people. I wanted to find out about Patterson's health before I voted. "How is Patterson? Can he die today?" I asked the doctors. At ten in the morning I was told that he could not die that day. So I told my supporters to go around to the polls and vote. I was in my office at eleven o'clock on election day, and Dr. Cairn said that there had been a great change in Patterson's condition. He would not live the night out. I called a meeting of the city committee. We had the stickers ready and decided to use them at once.

Another indication of the unity and precision of the Philadelphia party organization is revealed by an examination of the 1913 primary vote for candidates for the municipal courts. There were 142 candidates of a non-partisan ballot, 18 of whom were to be nominated. The organization got 14 of the places; independents won the other four.

The candidates were arranged in alphabetical order on the ballot, but it appears that alphabetical voting was of no importance at all. The order of the successful nominees follows: 17th, 24th, 33rd, 44th, 48th, 51st (high man on the ballot), 66th, 68th, 85th, 93rd, 112th, 118th, 131st, 132nd, 138th, 142nd.

In the election that followed the organization centered its efforts on electing nine of the 18 nominees. It succeeded in placing seven in office; one of these, along with two others, had been supported by the Committee of One Hundred and the press.

Another source of Bill Vare's strength was exactly that to which Boies Penrose's friends always ascribed his great power as a politician—"brains." As one of his friends put it, "Bill Vare was the most astute of the three brothers—he thinks carom shots ahead. He won't only think of getting Smith's vote, but know how to get Jones's vote through Smith, and Brown's vote through Jones and so on. Just like playing chess when you look half a dozen moves ahead." When George Vare died, many political observers thought that the Vare family had lost its most gifted member; between that time (1908) and 1922, opinion was nearly unanimous in proclaiming that Ed Vare was Caesar, and that Bill was just Ed's younger brother. But one of those who questioned this

estimate was Edwin Vare himself. He never underestimated the
political shrewdness and sagacity of brother Bill. When called
upon to decide a political question, he would always drawl, "Well,
I'll see what Bill thinks about this first." Some of his friends
thought that this was make-believe, but I do not think so. (However, the big brother had his lordly moments. Once when he was
being interviewed by newspapermen in his office in the Betz Building, he was irritated by his younger brother's continually walking
around the room. "Hey, Bill," he shouted, "sit down!" and Bill,
like all regulars in political or military life, obeyed.)

Vare always had an unusual faculty for sensing the drift of
sentiment and opinion, or noting the crux of a situation. When
he was uncertain, he often got in associates or outsiders, and discussed matters with them. One of his close friends said to me:

> He believes in getting the view of friends or outsiders on political
> matters often. He will send for me or some party official and ask,
> "What do you think about this?" From time to time he will get
> people that have no personal interest in these matters at all—
> people who don't know anything about it at all. In this way he
> gets the pulse of the people. It is a sort of guide to him. Vare terms
> this practice his "open door to the public." "I am sincerely con-
> vinced," he asserted, "that any man who wishes to make headway
> in public life must brush elbows with the people or otherwise he
> will fail."[6]

This ability to read the "signs of the times" (Vare's term for
drifts in public sentiment), as well as his political acumen in party
strategy, was effectively revealed in 1912-15 when he forced the
nomination of Brumbaugh for governor. At that time the senator-
ship and the gubernatorial office were both to be filled. Penrose
was, of course, the candidate for the United States Senate; and
he was against Vare and the Vare organization. Vare foresaw the
re-election fight that Penrose would have on his hands. As he
analyzed the situation:

> Not only was the 1914 election the first direct election of senators
> by the people, but Roosevelt had personally widened the breach
> between his followers and Penrose [T. R. had sent Elihu Root, his

secretary of state, to Philadelphia to make a speech for the purpose
of "purifying" the political conditions in Philadelphia].[7] Moreover,
the independents of the state had been restive for years under
Penrose's leadership, and only four years previously his candidate
for governor had but narrowly escaped defeat, while two other
important state offices had been lost in 1911. I pointed out to Ed
that Penrose could not get started in his efforts to force a candidate of his and McNichol's on the Republican ticket without
a solid Philadelphia behind him, as at the last election, Roosevelt
had polled 450,000 votes to 400,000 for Wilson, and with Taft a
poor third. Then I showed him the present trend of the country
favored the choice of educators in public affairs. Wilson, a
Democrat, had been elected president; of only three Republicans
from Ohio in Congress, two of these, Simeon D. Fess and Frank
Willis, had been educators. I then asked Ed to name the most
prominent school name in Pennsylvania and he immediately
replied "Brumbaugh." "He's the man for us," I said. My brother
agreed with me. [Martin G. Brumbaugh was superintendent of
Philadelphia public schools, an able man, an effective speaker, and
probably 30,000 teachers in the state knew him, or thought they
did. For these reasons Vare counted him "the strongest candidate
the Republicans could name, as he would attract thousands of
independents who had left the Taft ticket two years before and
would put the party back on its feet in the state."]

Some time later Ed and I called at Penrose's office. McNichol
and William E. Crow were there when we entered.

"Jim," I said to McNichol, "we have another candidate."

"Who is it?"

"Brumbaugh," I said. Penrose entered at this time and Mc-
Nichol told him what I had said. Penrose looked sour, but made
no declaration at the time.[8]

Vare had done much undercover work early in the campaign.
Six months before the fight started, he had Brumbaugh in the
field making speeches before school and other civic groups which
later passed resolutions for him. The state organization leaders
had smiled, for they had not known what Vare was doing. They
had laughed when Vare said, "I am for Brumbaugh." But Vare
gave publicity to his position on a gubernatorial candidate, and
Brumbaugh strength developed overnight. Vare took a poll of
the preferences of the congressional delegation; and fourteen of the
sixteen Republican members declared for Brumbaugh. "My

brother Ed got in touch with W. Harry Baker, secretary of the state committee, and informed him of the tally," Vare said. Within ten days he had forced Brumbaugh on Penrose, for Vare said, "If he is not for Brumbaugh, I am not for Penrose. If he wants to go back without a fight he supports Brumbaugh." Penrose saw the handwriting on the wall and accepted the schoolteacher to avoid a costly and uncertain fight. Moreover, John R. K. Scott of Philadelphia was named congressman at large as a further concession to the Vares. Twenty years later Vare was still proud of his political coup and boasted, "Brumbaugh won by the largest total ever recorded for a state candidate before woman suffrage."[9]

The Vares could always sacrifice immediate glory if the sacrifice meant ultimate political gain. In 1915 Ed declared that for the mayoralty candidate that year it was a case of "our Will, or fight." But at the last moment they switched to Thomas B. Smith, a move which was unaccountable to some at the time, for Smith was a Penrose-McNichol man. But it was soon clear that this apparent concession had strengthened the Vare position. Smith named many Vare men to important posts, which gave them virtual control of the city and county. Instead of waging a bitter fight to make Bill mayor, a fight which would only have weakened both sides, they worked for Smith's election; and thus they were in a strong position to ask for favors which would give them control of Philadelphia, for the first time.[10]

In 1924 Governor Pinchot was a candidate for delegate at large to a national convention. Up until four days before the primary election the governor thought that he had Vare's support. But on the Saturday preceding the Tuesday election Vare declared for Ralph B. Strassburger of Norristown, saying that recent utterances of Pinchot proved him disloyal to President Coolidge. The shortness of the time remaining cut the ground from under the governor's feet and he was defeated by 100,000 votes.

Another of Vare's opportune political moves was made by him in 1928 when he stole Mellon's thunder and put himself in the headlines of the great dailies by early declaring that Pennsylvania was going to support Herbert Hoover. Hoover received the nomination on the first ballot, and it is easily possible that he might never have received it had Vare remained silent. At that time Vare's right to a Senate seat was pending before the Senate. A grateful President might have helped a fellow Republican in distress, but Hoover, the engineer, did not understand such political niceties, and gave no sign that he had ever heard the name before.

(William Vare's declaration for Hoover in 1928 is reminiscent of the time when George Vare, as one of Durham's lieutenants, stole his chief's thunder by coming out in favor of Ashbridge for mayor in 1898. Coroner Ashbridge, who was a member of the Hog Combine, found that Martin, the head of the combine, was planning to throw him down in the nomination for mayor. George Vare took advantage of Durham's absence in New York to issue a statement for the papers announcing that he favored Ashbridge for mayor. With a candidate thus forced upon him, Durham was also inclined to issue a statement favoring Ashbridge. "But," Vare related, "my brother persuaded him not to do this, urging that this move might precipitate a general fight, while otherwise the opposition to Ashbridge would disintegrate of itself." Thus the Vares had the stage to themselves and were given credit for Ashbridge's election.)[11]

In 1930 there was a three-cornered fight for the gubernatorial nomination. Pinchot was running as a dry, Phillips as a wet, and Vare's candidate, Francis Shunk Brown, stood in between. Senator Vare told me that Brown failed to take a clear-cut position in this campaign because Charlie Hall, a rival city leader, insisted upon Brown's running on a referendum-idea platform. Vare himself wanted him to come out wet. This referendum idea cost the organization the nomination, for Phillips took enough votes from Brown to give Pinchot the election.

In the election that followed Vare supported Hemphill, the Democratic candidate. At this time 476,731 Philadelphians were registered as Republicans and only 36,599 as Democrats. Not since 1900 had any Democratic candidates received a majority of the votes in Philadelphia; however, the Republican candidate was an implacable enemy of the Vare organization, and his anger was both oral and written. In the final election Pinchot received

11,230 votes, and 356,881 votes were given to Hemphill. This election is additional testimony to the solidarity of the organization. There was one further fact that helped the Republican leaders, and that was Pinchot's dryness. In spite of the weight of the party tradition, many Philadelphians found it easier to vote for a wet Democrat than a dry Republican. (Senator X, powerful leader of the X Ward, tells this story about himself. "Knowing how my people felt about Gifford Pinchot, I was afraid that he would not get a single vote in one of my divisions. I did not want any zero divisions in this election for fear it might lead to an investigation. I started to ask one or two of my friends to vote for Pinchot, but when I saw the expression on their faces, I gave up. I voted for the Governor myself. The next day the committeeman in my neighborhood said, 'Look, boss, some son of a bitch around here voted for Pinchot!' ")

Another evidence of Vare's political astuteness was his way of making up a county ticket—in distributing the places to the men who were entitled to them. When he got through with a ticket composed of eight, eighteen, or twenty places (and at the time when magistrates and judges were elected, there were more), an analysis of the ticket geographically or on the basis of religion or nationality would show that from a party leader's standpoint, everybody had been taken care of. Vare could do for himself what only proportional representation could do for the people. Some of the places were given to Catholics—"A large religious organization is entitled to recognition." And it would not be wise to ignore all the Israelites and expect them to be satisfied. The same was true of the colored people and the Italians, Swedes, Slavs, and other nationality groups. During the last two years of his life Councilman Trainer and Senator Sam Salus and County Commissioner Clark helped him to frame a ticket, although Vare's closest friends insisted that he had the final say; there is no doubt that he relied more on others then that he had ever had to before.

I have already mentioned the 1926 campaign of Vare, but I shall comment on it again here, since Vare, largely because of the remarkable campaign he directed, scored there one of the most extraordinary political victories ever recorded in Pennsylvania.

The odds against Vare were the sort that would have made a lesser man hesitate and on second thought turn back. Vare clear-headedly saw the obstacles in the long race before him; but with his Philadelphia machine functioning as a harmonious whole, he felt the time was ripe for him to seek to realize his almost lifelong ambition—a seat in the United States Senate and the leadership of the Republican party in Pennsylvania. Vare, the precinct politician, who had risen to power through a political machine which stood only for political corruption and bossism in the minds of millions of Pennsylvanians, to gain the prize he sought had to accomplish the defeat of his two powerful opponents. One, a wealthy aristocrat and a distinguished lawyer, Senator George Wharton Pepper, was backed by two of the greatest political and financial powers in Pennsylvania: Mr. Grundy in the east, and the mighty Mellon machine in the west, which controlled the state Republican organization. Thus Senator Pepper had the support of the banks, the railroads, the public utilities, the large industralists, and the great newspapers in Pennslyvania. Vare's other opponent was the aristocratic governor of the state, Gifford Pinchot, the graduate of two universities, the possessor of much inherited wealth, who had gained national fame as a reformer and as a Roosevelt Republican. He was the Progressive crusader against political bossism who had managed to build up a strong organization of his own through his power of appointment. Moreover, according to Harry A. Mackey (Vare's campaign manager), Pinchot was "the greatest publicity man in the world. He can get a front page story, first because of his prestige as governor; next, because of what he says, and he is not altogether limited by facts in his statements; and the way he says it gives a news value to his statements, so that every newspaper in the state is bound to carry it as a front page story, regardless of their political affiliations."[12]

Perhaps the greatest obstacle in Vare's path was the fact that outside of Philadelphia, he was without an organization. That is, he had an organization which would promote his candidacy in only 1,400 of the 8,000 precincts in the state. Moreover, his name was known in the state only as the term "Vareism" had been coined to signify boss-ridden politics. He had been in Pittsburgh only five times in his life. As he told the Senate committee, "My political experience has largely—in fact, almost entirely, been confined to Philadelphia."[13] On the other hand, both Pinchot and Pepper were well known and had many friends and interests in the state, which they could rely upon. Pinchot had fifty thousand officeholders whom he could appoint and discharge at will, and over whose salaries he was sole arbiter.[14] Pepper, besides being backed by the Mellon machine, had a state-wide political organization built up through federal patronage dealt out to some twenty-five thousand people.[15]

"So my proposition was how I could get to the people of Pennslyvania with whom I had never met before, and in whose counties I had never before been invited to even make an address, outside of Philadelphia. That is the general background of what I found conditions to be after I announced my candidacy."[16]

Having reached the decision to announce his candidacy no matter what the cost might prove to be, Vare demonstrated his political acumen and at the same time his lesser ability to judge the character of men, by his first move. He chose as campaign manager the Honorable Harry Mackey, an astute politician (who as chairman of the workmen's compensation board for eight years had been into every nook and corner of Pennsylvania, and had been in close contact with three great groups of people: 300,000 employers, the 3,500,000 workmen who had benefited from the board, and all the insurance underwriters of the state). Although Mackey was to be the first of a series of palace intriguers to reach for Vare's crown, he was well fitted for the job that Vare had assigned him, and he could draw on his wide acquaintanceship in setting up a state organization for the Vare candidacy.[17]

Vare's first problem was to find an effective message to carry to the voter. "The thing to do is to find what the majority of them [the voters] want and give it to them" was the way he analyzed the situation. In 1926 the citizens of Pennsylvania were smugly content with Coolidge prosperity. Vare knew that what the majority in 1926 wanted most, was not honest and efficient government which would save money for the taxpayers. What the prosperous nation wanted was a release from the 18th Amendment. More important, Philadelphia had just been put through the wringer by that hard-bitten marine, General Smedley D. Butler, in an effort to sop up its dampness, and the whole of Pennslyvania had felt the blow of the Snyder search-and-seizure law. Throughout the country there was a rising feeling against the prohibition amendment. William Vare felt the ground swell. He became the first important person in Pennsylvania to take an out-and-out wet position. Thus his message to the citizens of Pennsylvania could be summed up by the word "beer." He would, as he phrased it, "give an American his rights."

His decisive stand on the liquor question was one of the two most telling factors in his victory. "Beer was without doubt the factor which contributed most to my victory," Vare later wrote. Pepper hedged on the liquor question, with the purpose of winning support from the drys in some sections and from wringing wets in other counties. He was dry in Philadelphia and wet in Pittsburgh. He told the W.C.T.U. that he was whatever the state was. The Methodist preachers were not satisfied, and so he told them he was bone-dry. He wrote to the hotelkeepers, however, to tell them to vote for him instead of for a "radical dry" or "hysterical wet." Mackey described Pepper's effort to be dry in the east and wet in the west thus: ". . . he was wobbling from one side to the other, trying to dip in and get a little from both sides. He wobbled himself to defeat."[18]

Governor Pinchot, like Vare, did not straddle the issue. He came out strongly opposed to modification. But either he failed to read public sentiment aright or else he refused to compromise with his principles for the sake of political expediency. At any rate, his was the losing task of trying to make his record as an honest and efficient administrator, which he elaborately described in a campaign booklet of uninteresting proportions, as palatable to the electorate as the light wines and beer which Vare promised.

As no political organization except his own in Philadelphia was interested in the Vare candidacy, the job of getting together a temporary machine in the 6,660 unorganized precincts had to be done wholly through individual contacts—through the use of "key" men. To get Vare's name on the ballot required 100 signatures in each of ten counties, or 1,000 names in all.

I first addressed myself to the securing of those names [Mackey related to the Senate committee]. I put myself in communication with my friends in every county of the state, asking if they would assist me in circulating such a paper. I put myself in touch with every fraternal organization in Pennsylvania, through some representative men in Philadelphia, and asked each of them to take a hundred papers and send out through his friends in the counties . . . in about a week's time I had secured 300,000 signatures instead of the thousand that were really necessary and they were filed at Harrisburg.

I decided to get a large number of names because I would take those names as groups in the various counties and from them I would try—by the process of elimination I would try—to get some active fellow to be our county leader. I wanted no old politicians; I wanted nobody with a lot of political scars, or prejudices against him; I wanted some live young fellows who would just get around and get to work; because I knew the problem before me.[19]

Mackey's directions to Congressman Morin, his lieutenant in the west whose task it was to organize the seventeen counties in that part of the state, illustrates the way he picked his organization. "I gave him a list of names of men with whom I had been in communication and asked him to send for them to come in and size them up and see if he thought they were good enough material to build an organization around, and to report to me."[20]

A political alliance was also made to strengthen the organization that Mackey and Vare were fast setting up. "Political expediencies of the time," wrote Vare, "required that alliances be made with partisan elements of the party, and for this reason my candidacy was linked with that of Edward E. Beidleman of Harrisburg, a former lieutenant governor who sought the governorship of the state."[21] Vare, by promising to deliver 400,000 votes for Beidleman, allied himself with him, and also aligned with Arthur James of Luzerne County and James Woodward of Allegheny County. By mutual cooperation and a trade of votes it was hoped to carry the state.[22]

Thus Vare was provided with a temporary state-wide machine. Although a rather loosely connected one, his organization had the advantage of being flexible. Vare also knew the advantages of centralized responsibility and control. Therefore, he gave Mackey complete charge of the campaign. "I had no associates," Mackey explained; "I was the whole thing as far as the management of our campaign was concerned. I had nobody to confer with. Whatever was done was done on my judgment. . . ."[23] One of the conditions of my appointment was that I was to be the sole arbitrator in all matters; that there was no supreme court to be over me; and that I had to act quickly and had to act upon my own judgment and that I was to surround myself with men and women of my own selection."[24]

His appointees were in no sense a conference committee which might delay necessary action while reaching a decision. They were merely administrative aides to carry out Mackey's particular orders to them. All of his chief lieutenants (with the exception of Thomas F. Watson, the treasurer whom Vare himself had picked; George F. Holmes, a newspaperman who had been political editor of the Philadelphia *North American* for years, and who was put in charge of state publications, and Paul M. Gottlieb, who took care of the publicity) were picked because of their positions of leadership among powerful social or political groups in the state.

> We had to bring in all the various elements of the community [he explained]. I secured the services of Dr. Leon Felderman, who was county chairman of the Veterans of Foreign Wars, and I put him in there [he related, in testifying before the senate committee]:
> *Chairman.* What for?
> *Mr. Mackey.* To secure the cooperation of the soldiers.
> *Chairman.* What was he to do?
> *Mr. Mackey.* To mingle among the veterans of the various wars.
> *Chairman.* I mean, did he have any position on the committee?
> *Mr. Mackey.* Nothing except that, sir; he was to confine his activities entirely to the veterans.
> *Senator King.* What did you call him; just a member of the committee?
> *Mr. Mackey.* No; I had no committee. These were my appointees, my aides.
> Then I secured the services of Mrs. Blanche A. Bellak, and she opened up one of the rooms [in the headquarters building furnished Vare by Albert Greenfield] and called it a mothers' committee. She had been the head of the War Mothers. Therefore, I placed her in charge of talking with the large number of mothers.

She formed a committee of mothers who were impressed with the fact that the society was being injured very much because of the inconsistencies and hypocrisy of the Volstead Act.[25]

Then I invited Mrs. H. A. Sinnamon, a member of the regular organization, as vice-chairman, and I asked her to take charge of the women's auxiliary. She was to organize the women. . . . Then I had a friend, a young man who lost a leg in France, who was still on crutches. He opened up a room there and put himself in contact with the service men. . . . Then we had a business men's committee, which was formed late in the campaign. I have the names of that committee here and the occupations of 1,000 of the most prominent businessmen of Pennsylvania; and that was headed by Frank H. Tugt, president of the Metropolitan Trust Company.

Then Mr. Pepper boasted that he had all the lawyers sewed up; but I knew several lawyers and I had a lawyer's committee of 200, and I placed Major L. B. Schofield in charge of the lawyer's committee.

This was the organization whose task it was to present Vare so favorably to the voters of Pennsylvania that they would make him their senator.

With a temporary state organization knit together, competent assistants picked, and the machinery set for the distribution of campaign material, the Vare leadership launched one of the most extensive and spectacular publicity campaigns Pennsylvania ever witnessed. For skillful direction and for thoroughness of coverage, the Vare-Mackey directed campaign might well serve as a handbook for anyone desiring to make a fight for public office.

Vare's campaign was to be waged without benefit of the press. "I suppose it took me only 24 hours," Vare explained, "to find that virtually the united press of the state was for my two opponents. I should say probably that the percentage was about 6 to 1; in other words, about one out of every seven was for Governor Pinchot. The other six were for Senator Pepper."[26] Thus Vare had to appeal directly to the people of Pennsylvania. "We cannot expect to get any newspaper support," Vare told Mackey. "We could not get any news items. So we agreed upon an extensive letter writing campaign."[27]

To blanket the state with his personal message was a sizable job. Pennsylvania comprised some 44,000 square miles of territory and contained 10 million people, of whom roughly 4 million were able to vote. To these 4 million voters approximately 9 million pieces of literature were to be distributed before the primary. Of this flood of mail 680,000 pieces were to be personal letters sent out with two-cent stamps. (Vare did not take advantage of his franking privilege in waging his campaign.)[28]

Only prominent people in various groups within the state were to receive a letter. Their influence over their own group was depended upon to spread the good word. To each different group a new appeal was made, an appeal that would be near the heart of the person receiving it. To attract votes in the rural sections (where resentment against the Vare machine was strongest) he sent 250,000 letters to farmers.

"I was born on a farm in the lower part of Philadelphia," Vare told the Senate committee. "As a boy I went to work when I was 12 years of age. I had a picture of my old farmhouse; and I sent a copy of the old farmhouse to as many farmers as I could get lists of. I had supported very much farm legislation during the 14 years I was a member of the House, and, coupled with the fact of my early experience on the farm, I felt that the farmers of Pennsylvania were entitled to know that I had first hand knowledge of their wants and requirements."[29]

Following perusal of the personal letter, the farmers could read "An Address to the Farmers" and a pamphlet entitled "Why the Farmer Should be For Vare," enclosed with the letters.[30]

"In addition to that, as a contractor I was familiar with road construction. I knew the kinds of roads that would be the most durable, and I sent out many letters to automobile users, etc., those who would be interested in good roads. . . . I had always taken a great interest in the public school system of Philadelphia; I sent a letter to very many people connected with the public school system of the State."[31]

I might add that I belong to many organizations of one kind or another, and wherever I could secure any part of a list of the memberships, I wrote letters. [Among them were Vaux Lodge, St. John's Chapter, No. 232, Mary Commandery, No. 36, Philadelphia Consistory, LuLu Temple, Ancient Order Mystic Shrine, Philadelphia Aerie No. 42, Fraternal Order of Eagles, Patriotic

Order Sons of America, Philadelphia Lodge No. 2, Benevolent Protective Order of Elks, Loyal Order of Moose, Improved Order of Red Men, Friendly Sons of St. Patrick, Clover Club, Manufacturers Club, National Press Club of Washington, D.C., Harvey Cedars Club, Young Republicans, Union Republican Clubs of South Philadelphia.] So I did make a very extensive personal campaign, for the reason that I had absolutely no way of presenting my case to the people of Pennsylvania; and I had announced my candidacy and I felt that I wanted to make the very best possible effort that I could. As a result of that extensive letter writing campaign, I personally expended seventy-one thousand and some odd dollars, I do not recall. Those are round figures.[32]

Besides the thousands of letters, newspaper advertising played a major role in the campaign. Although newspaper editors might refuse to print stories of Vare's activities in their news columns, the business department had no scruples about taking his paid advertising publicity. It cost him $27,712.74 to get his message into the English newspapers. And to get his message to the vast group of foreign-born in the state—a group whose support had always been a major factor in the organization's success at the polls—$34,016.07 was spent in foreign and interracial newspapers.[33]

Most of the advertising was carried in the dailies and weeklies out in the state, for the Philadelphia organization could be relied upon to bring in the votes in Philadelphia without the aid of newspaper advertising. However, there were several exceptions worth noting. The Business Men's Committee of One Hundred endorsed Vare's election in the Philadelphia *Inquirer* because he was a businessman who could be trusted to represent the business interests of Pennsylvania in the Senate. On another occasion the Vare forces were obliged to advertise to stop a whispering campaign that the Philadelphia organization was deserting Vare. Throughout Pennsylvania the voters were being told, "Now, just wait. Just wait. There is going to be a great break in the Rebublican organization at Philadelphia."[34] To stamp out this rumor once and for all, Mackey organized

probably what was the most remarkable meeting that was ever held in Philadelphia . . . we arranged for a meeting in Elks Hall for the ward leaders, to bring all of their workers, men and women, into one meeting, and I arranged to bring the county leaders down there whom we selected, and put them on display. I had the lawyers on the platform, and had the women's committee, the soldiers' committee, and I had the county leaders, and then I had all of these men in the old convention form, sitting by wards at the head of their delegations, men and women; only by tickets; not a public meeting, but only active workers, each holding a ticket issued by his ward leader. We had 5,000 seated inside and many more there trying to get in.

Then I began to put them on display. I called upon every ward leader to stand up and tell what majority he was going to give for the Beidleman-Vare ticket, and they all stated their majorities; but they underestimated. The majorities were going to be 174,000 according to that meeting, and Mr. Vare's majority was 228,000.[35]

Each ward leader also signed his name on the dotted line, pledging himself to support Vare. This was then drawn up into an advertisement, with the facsimile of the signatures signed under the printed statement.

Perhaps the most clever and effective bit of newspaper publicity was the advertisement which boldly attempted to redefine Vareism, and rid the word of its evil connotation:

"From Philadelphia to Pittsburgh there was a united assault by both of the candidates upon Mr. Vare, picturing him as a low-bred man. You would have thought he was a thug, a product of the underworld, and they began to use the term 'Vareism' as meaning something loathesome, and therefore, we caused that to be put in to show what 'Vareism' meant in his home town," Mackey related. The advertisement was effectively laid out with pictures of the Abigail Vare Methodist-Episcopal Church, the Abigail Vare Public School, the E. H. Vare Junior High School, and the George A. Vare playgrounds. According to the advertisement, what Vareism stood for was "here shown in stone and brick and mortar, monuments of unselfish endeavor directed for the good of the community. . . . A Church—a School where the foreign-born are Americanized—a High School that better fits the boys and girls for the duties that await them—a Playground where sunshine and fresh air give new life to pent-up children in congested districts. These four contributions to a community's well-being represent what 'Vareism' really means."[36]

Tons of circulars, pamphlets, and cards were scattered broadcast through the state. Vare's platform, which Mackey called "the most popular thing in the whole campaign," was printed in fourteen different languages and 1,300,000 copies were widely distributed. The slogan "Give an American his rights" was to be the rallying cry of the campaign. For Vare knew that there were few better ways of attracting voters' attention and interest than by means of slogans and catch-words. And he needed no psychologist to tell him that to persuade the voter to act in the desired manner on election day, he had first to capture his attention and interest. The biggest sign ever put up in an American city, which appealed to the voter to "Give an American his rights," was constructed on a Broad Street building, so that "everybody going to or coming away from the Reading Railroad had to look at it." "And," Mackey added, "they came from miles around to see it."[37] Into the coal regions were sent 10,000 smart tricolor-bordered cards reading on one side: "Give an American his rights. The Issue: Personal Liberty and Self-government versus Money Power, Mellon-Pepper-Fisher-Grundy." The reverse side of the card declared: "Vare knows no 'boss.' He owns himself and only takes orders from the plain people, for he is one of them."[38] The *Sunday Dispatch,* a Vare organ, with admirable alliteration declared in a headline: "MELLONISM, MONEY, AND MISREPRESENTATION PLUS PEPPER, PRESSMUZZLING AND PREVARICATION EQUALS VARE, VINDICATION AND VICTORY." Four hundred and seventy-five thousand sample ballots were sent throughout the state with the names of the Vare ticket checked on them as an aid to the voter. In Mackey's opinion 225,000 votes could be changed in ten minutes by sending a marked ballot to 1,492 voting precincts.[39] Mass rallies were held throughout the state. Committeemen trundled speakers about evenings, speaking from bandstands and automobile tonneaus—all in the effort to get in personal contact with the voters.[40] This was the day when most politicians had yet to learn the value of the radio as a campaign instrument, yet Mackey alone made two radio speeches each day during the campaign. Perhaps one of the most effective radio speeches given was that of Vare's daughter, Beatrice. To counteract the charges of "Vareism," "contractor government" and "corruption of the ballot" hurled by the opposition, Beatrice went on the air to speak for her "dear daddy." She told how Vare got his own breakfast in the mornings so that he would not have to disturb Mrs. Vare. She described him as "a big man doing big things and remembering all the while that, although the big things make life much greater, it is the little things which often make it much sweeter." She told how the "dearest daddy in all the world" kept the vigil beside his dying daughter's bed, years before, and how he "wept, and watched, and prayed." Thus the sentimental voter saw Vare, not as the ruthless boss of a city but as the benevolent father and the believer in the Christian God.[41]

Mackey, describing his political cleverness in directing Vare's campaign, indirectly took the credit for winning the primary and general election for Vare. But it is the Philadelphia organization, whose machinery Vare had geared to such perfect harmony, which must be given a large share of the credit for the Vare nomination and election. It was this faithful group which piled up the 337,944 votes in Vare's home city—votes which enabled Vare to win out in the tri-cornered fight. For he carried only one county outside of his own, and that was Beidleman's.

How effectively his machine functioned is shown by the product it turned out at the polls. The 4th Ward, of which the Honorable Samuel Salus, president of the Pennsylvania senate, was the leader, turned in a vote of 4,547 for Vare; 45 for Pepper; and 3 for Pinchot. In the 2nd Ward 7,203 votes were given to Vare in contrast to Pepper's 165 and Pinchot's 31. In the 5th, Pinchot received 14, Pepper 39 and Vare 4,489. Such figures indicate, of course, that there were many "zero" wards where Pinchot did not receive a vote. When Mackey explained to Chairman Reed that Philadelphia's first twenty wards were the "melting pot of America—all nationalities," Reed, with pardonable curiosity, replied, "I am not at all reflecting on these people, but I am curious how such patriotic people as you described should be so com-

pletely of one mind, when they come from so many countries."[42]
Thus it was that a 228,000 majority was piled up in Philadelphia,
which gave Vare enough votes to carry the state. He was in no
sense the popular choice of the whole state; he is best described,
perhaps, as the candidate of his own machine.[43]

IV

In spite of the terrific opposition with which he was almost
steadily confronted, from one camp or the other, Vare was not a
vindictive person; he never enjoyed the luxury of a personal
grudge. He was so interested in the success of the Republican
party that he would accept a man who had tried to injure him
rather than permit the Republican party to be weakened. He could
rarely afford retaliation; it might weaken his position. Charles B.
Hall, former president of the City Council, was long Vare's in-
veterate enemy. In 1931, as I have said, he tried to destroy Vare
when Vare was gravely ill. He failed, and a few days later he
himself was stricken with an illness from which he did not recover. But when the slate was made up in Philadelphia for members of the legislature and state committeemen, and Vare could
have displaced every man that was endorsed by Hall, he is reported to have said, "My friends thought it was very wrong of my
enemies to try to wrest power from me when I was extremely ill;
now I am not going to displace a single person that was loyal to
Hall when he was in health, until he either dies or recovers his
health." That is not to say that he was never ruthless. Part of his
strategy was, of course, his ruthlessness; no successful organization
boss can be anything but ruthless on occasion; he must break
those who oppose him within his organization. To quote one of
his most discerning fellow politicians:

> His political enemies, of course, would say that he pursues his
> political career with utter disregard for the happiness and welfare
> of those who oppose him. This may be too harsh a criticism. I

have known him to conciliate his political opponents and add them to his organization, and on the other hand I have seen him pursue and ruin their political careers. With some this would be called cruelty in the extreme. This judgment must depend upon the point of view of the one affected. I have seen him destroy ward leaders but at the same time create others to take their places. I have seen him make District Attorneys, judges, and other officials and eventually destroy them. In other words, his whole life has been marked by making men who will serve him, and destroying those who refused to do so. I presume that this is the history of every successful machine politician. Those who are affiliated with him would call this leadership, and others would hold it up as evidence of the cruelty of a machine boss who would crush a man of strong personal convictions who has the temerity to pursue his own way regardless of the consequences at the hands of a political boss.

Even the humblest know that "party treachery does not pay." An old precinct captain, in describing the Burke-McAleer fight for Congress in 1900, in an aside told of the fate of a politician who was misguided enough to support the Democratic candidate:

A well-known Republican ward leader of the district, who was regarded like Caesar's wife, above suspicion, did a turn-turtle at the eleventh hour, was caught at it, and his ward held in line for Burke despite his defection. And although that desertion occurred 31 years ago and the leader in question has remained in politics and has made repeated efforts to win his way back to party confidence, he has never since been a factor of any real importance, whether in his ward or in the city. Party treachery doesn't pay. Men may thrive at it for a time. In the end they're sent to Coventry and shut out from all party consideration.[44]

The overwhelming majority of the members of the Vare organization in 1933, and this included more than 75 per cent of the politicians in Philadelphia, said that one could get further ahead in politics by annoying Vare than by completely acquiescing to his orders. Of course, James Hazlett or Jimmie Clark or Miss Marion Pyle would not advocate so radical a procedure—they achieved high place by obediently carrying out orders. Nor was this strategy to be recommended to weak or uncertain persons, lest they find themselves thrown overboard like rotten apples. But if one had inherent qualities of leadership—something to deliver— one could capture Vare's attention by attacking him or his organization.

When Blankenberg was mayor, a certain member of his cabinet, an outstanding independent who had studied politics at Princeton under Woodrow Wilson, discovered that the voting lists were padded with phantom names. This director secured the names of the phantoms and arranged to have these names for a given division in the hands of a policeman who in spite of the Shern Law to the contrary was ordered to be at the polling place in his division and arrest the individuals who came to vote the phantom names. The police kept the phantoms away, and inadvertently tried to frighten away some real men like George Wharton Pepper. Dave Lane, the peerless leader, charged not only that the presence of the police at the polls had been illegal but that all the rights of man had been trampled upon. The director was ordered to appear before the grand jury for "violating the laws of his country." I shall give the story here as it was told to me by the director himself.

The day that a notice of this Grand Jury investigation got into the newspaper, I received a telephone call from William S. Vare. I immediately took off the receiver and with the same voice that all the Vares had, this voice said to me, "I suppose you know that you have been summoned before the Grand Jury. Are you frightened?" I said, "Not that I am aware of." "Well," said Vare, "you needn't be, but I'll tell you that if I were you, I would send for Harry Mackey. I think he has something to tell you that would interest you." I said that I would be very glad to do that. As soon as he hung up, I called Harry Mackey. I said, "Mackey, Vare says he thinks I would like to have a talk with you." Mackey said, "Yes, but we can't talk over the phone." I replied that no one wanted to do that; I said, "Come on over." Mackey said, "I'll be right over." Shortly after that he appeared at the office, and he said, "Director, I think all Mr. Vare wanted you to know was the fact that we have had a very careful study made of the Grand Jury, and we find out that almost all of them are Vare men; the leader comes from my ward. You have absolutely nothing to worry about; they have all had their orders to give you a clean slate. In addition to that we will keep you informed as to all that goes on within the Jury every day." Every night I would be called and told the whole works! (Of course, you know no one is supposed to know anything that goes on with the Jury. The funny part was I had another friend not in the organization who also knew someone on the Jury, and who would also report to me, and we would check up. Vare was absolutely truthful.) One day the time came that I was to appear. I was simply requested to appear—a man in a position of that kind is never summoned to court, but merely asked to appear; if he doesn't appear, I don't know what they would do. After the court had been in session for some days I received word that I was to appear that afternoon at 2:30. That morning my boy came in, and told me that Vare was on the phone. Vare said, "I understand that you have been asked to appear before the Grand Jury this afternoon. You're not afraid to go, are you? I think that you had better speak to Harry Mackey again." So Mackey came over again, and as he came in he took a piece of paper out of his pocket. He said, "I think I ought to tell you the kind of questions that they are apt to ask you. I thought maybe I could prepare you for it a little." He then read me 7, 8, 9, or 10 questions. "You could answer all of those, couldn't you?" I said, "No, there is one I will have to ask the Superintendent of Police." He said, "All right, ask him, and get it quick." I called the Superintendent of Police, and had the information in about 20 minutes. I said, "I don't see how they could ask me that question." "Well," he said, "I can see it, if you can't, and I think you had better know the answer." So of course I agreed. At the proper time I appeared before the Grand Jury and was duly sworn. The foreman of the Grand Jury put his hand in his pocket, and I recognized the piece of paper. I was asked those identical questions, and no others. After deliberating, the Grand Jury found that I was a scholar and a gentleman, and that I had acted solely to the views and best interests of my city. That day I was called up and congratulated by Vare.

To continue the director's account:

I know some years afterward he called me and asked me if he could put me up on the mountain. It was after I was Director, but near that time.

I was walking through City Hall one day and I met Jim Hazlett—a real politician. Jim said to me, "Why in the world don't you make up with Bill Vare?" I said, "What are you talking about? I'm not having any trouble with Bill Vare." He said, "You have a wonderful chance if you would play politics with Bill Vare. He is very fond of you." I said, "He must be." Jim said, "Now, don't be sarcastic; he is." I said, "What are you leading to?" "Well," he said, "are you willing to meet Bill Vare?" "Surely," I said, "but it is perfectly ridiculous; nothing will come of it. [Bill Vare was then a congressman.] All right, "I said, "I'll meet him." Jim asked me if I would come to his office. I said, "Certainly—any old time!" He said, "Where are you going to be this morning?" "In my office," I said. About ten or eleven o'clock I was asked if I would come around the next morning at ten o'clock. I was there at ten o'clock and Vare was there ahead of me. I was taken into an inner room, and he was sitting on a sofa.

He said, "X a lot of my friends say to me, why were you such a fool as to save that fellow X during the Grand Jury investigation? What was the big idea?" I say to them, "You fellows make me sick—you don't understand anything. Here is a young lawyer, he has no influence politically or any other way, but he is ambitious, and he wants to break into politics, just as you and I wanted to once." They say, "Why didn't he come to the Republicans?" I said, "He figured they have the big men—how could he get ahead there? The best thing to do and the only way for him was to make himself annoying. He gets into an independent organization and proceeds to be as annoying as he can. At first he did bother us a little in his own ward, but later on he became damned annoying, damned annoying! In fact he has become sufficiently powerful that we cannot ignore him any longer; and so I have sent for you to tell you that you have done what you set out to do. You're not the kind of a fool that is going to knock his head against a stone wall all his life. What do you want? Do you want to be Mayor?—you can be Mayor—I can put you there. Do you want to go to congress? I can send you." "Well,' I said, "that is all very nice and very pretty, but you overlook the fact that I am not interested in politics anymore. I must earn my bread." He said, "You must stay in." But I told him that I should not have accepted his offer if I had stayed in any way; I said that a man doesn't get anywhere by going after the thing in a mercenary way, and I regarded his proposition as that."

This story, needless to say, not only reveals how absolute was Vare's control but also reveals the maestro in an attempt, here unsuccessful, to win the allegiance of an independent.

V

Vare once said to me, "Any success I may have made is due to three things: industry, good home training—I had a good Christian mother—and a sound public-school education." And then he repeated, "I have lived a very industrious life." His tempo before he was stricken was about like this: He would often get down to his office, having come all the way from Atlantic City, before nine o'clock; when his secretary arrived by nine, he might find that Vare had already talked to twenty persons. He would call them on the phone early in the morning; and he would keep on seeing people all day, even into the late afternoon. He once told a friend of his that the trouble was that there were not eight days in a week instead of seven. The friend replied that the only thing for the Senator to do was to work all night. "That wouldn't do, for I work all night now," Vare answered. This same friend added: "I have seen him work until 2 A.M. and then get up at 5 A.M. and get a train for Washington. I have met him in a streetcar at 1 A.M. coming from Harrisburg. "Why don't you go home and get acquainted with your family?" I asked. "That is what I am going to do now. I expect to get up at five and go to Washington," he replied. He would get home from Washington at midnight and take an early morning train to Harrisburg. Even his most bitter and vocal enemies agreed that he had almost superhuman energy. As one of them said, "There are no limits to his political activity." A second opponent of his said, "He has tremendous energy—his history shows that. He started in with nothing—a poor working boy on an ash cart—and by his energy, ability, and resourcefulness he has reached his present position, whether you like it or not."

Apart from his natural good health, Vare was fairly temperate in his personal habits. He never was a great drinker and very rarely permitted himself to come under the influence of liquor. When he was in the company of people who drank he sometimes drank, but it was invariably a modest drink. One of his friends told me, "Men never arrive at political prominence

who drink heavy—the game is too deep and too strenuous."
However, there were rare times—even since the dire days of
August, 1928—when Senator Vare could gulp down a half water
glass full of whiskey, and without blinking. Vare said that he
used to be a heavy smoker. One time his mother came home and
the place was full of smoke. She said she didn't like smoking,
and wanted him to give it up. He was a comparatively young man
at the time; he did as she wished and held to it.

There never was anything loquacious or demagogic about
Vare; his energy was not of that kind. In public or with people
he was generally silent. His invariable response to newspapermen
was "I have no statement to make." And when his final defeat
was encompassed in June, 1934, Vare, slipping from the city for
his winter home in Florida, stepped out of the Philadelphia political scene forever with the same remark: "I have no statement
to make." It was only to his cronies that he occasionally used to
talk for long stretches of time.

That he thoroughly enjoyed discussing his political maneuvers
and experiences, however, he convincingly proved to me when I
went to interview him in 1930, before his illness had completely
weakened him.

"Get out—the gentleman is here at my request!" Vare said
to his wife at the beginning of the interview, just as I had risen
to answer her query, "Who are you—are you a newspaperman
too?" He and I were sitting on the simple porch of his spacious
Atlantic City home, in August, 1930. We had just begun talking
about his life in politics when Mrs. Vare asked me this through
a screen door nearby. She quickly turned away before I could
reply; the Senator continued to speak. To him his command was
only a parenthetical remark; to me it demonstrated that he was
the boss of the family even though he is sometimes referred to
as merely the titular boss of the Philadelphia organization.[45]

About an hour later, a prominent judge from City Hall arrived. He was entertained by Beatrice Vare at the far end of the
porch; I could see them, but Senator Vare was facing the ocean.
A half hour later I mentioned that the judge was there and asked
if I should call some other time. "Stay right where you are. You

are the only person I have an engagement with tonight." He then called his daughter, asked who the visitor was, and upon learning that it was his friend, the Honorable Leopold Glass, asked to have him join us. We were introduced and were barely seated, before Vare shouted, "Now, Professor, go right on with your questions." I observed him ten or twelve times in public and private and I never saw him so enthusiastic as he was in the midst of these pleasant questions on politics. His manner at this point suggested that he relished the idea of showing Judge Glass the fine grasp that he had of his subject (and probably of the interviewer too!).

Ward leaders generally would describe him by saying, "He is a very shrewd man. He does a lot of listening and lets the other fellow talk." One of Philadelphia's most respected judges who was a lifelong friend of Vare's said once, "He is a great listener—he does not believe in doing a lot of talking. When you are talking to him he may not seem to be listening, but every word that is being said is finding a place in the back of his head." A close relative of Vare's said, "One of his greatest characteristics is that he is the greatest listener I know, and he knows how to keep his mouth shut! He may be insulted in the newspapers and severely criticized by his opponents, but in the face of this he keeps his mouth shut and does not reply until he gets good and ready."

A political lieutenant of Vare's who was well past middle life, and had known Vare for many years, one day remarked, "He is a queer fellow. He will hear something about you. He won't say anything at the time. Later, a month or so later, he will unexpectedly ask, 'Tom, how did you come to do so and so?' You have forgotten all about the matter. You tell him the truth before you know what you are doing."

So the luxury of telling a much disliked person what he thought of him was one that Vare rarely indulged in. However, he and his advisers nodded when Major Schofield called on Vare at Atlantic City once, in order to get the leader's support for District Attorney Monaghan. Following the conference, Vare gave the newspaper the following statement.[46]

I have been prompted to talk a little about Monaghan. I have been requested to recommend to the Republican Organization of Philadelphia, and through them the people of Philadelphia, the renomination and re-election of John Monaghan as District Attorney of Philadelphia.

But since I have returned from my recent trip, I have been waited upon by very many people, many of whom were members of the Philadelphia bar.

These members of the bar have advised me that Monaghan has not shown any rare ability as District Attorney, either in the prosecution of cases or in the administrative work of the office.

In addition I have been reminded by a number of callers that the Republican Organization of Philadelphia has taken care of Monaghan since 1896.

Also from a personal standpoint, I surely am under no obligation to Mr. Monaghan, if personal obligation should be allowed to enter into the proposition.

When I was practically at death's door, in fact my family and physicians thought I could not live, Mr. Monaghan called on me and I said to him, "I already have four physicians and I want to add you to my staff, making it one more. There is one thing that you can do for me. If you will do it, it will save my life, and that is for you to say a kind word in favor of retention of Harry C. Davis as Director of Public Safety. No charges have ever been filed against him, and everyone around City Hall knows he is not only highly efficient but also strictly honest."

(Monaghan did nothing to save Davis, who was removed by the mayor as director of public safety. Monaghan's assistant, Lemuel Schofield, was given the director's job.)

During the next few days critical editorials appeared in the Philadelphia newspapers concerning the boss's attitude toward an important public office. But Vare said no more. He had said too much; he had said more than he ever would say publicly again.

Another source of Vare's strength was the forthright, almost blunt sort of personal honesty he possessed. His contempt for hypocrisy won him the respect of even his avowed enemies. The Philadelphia *Record* declared editorially:

Whatever his critics may say about him, William S. Vare was consistent. He was no hypocrite. He traveled under no false colors. He never pretended to be a reformer. Neither did he dis-

guise the fact that the power of his political organization came
first and last where he was concerned. Now that he has passed
on, the Record has no intention of indulging in hypocrisy either.
We respected Vare because he was not a pretender—but we fought
him because he stood for political principles which we regard as
abhorrent in a free democracy.

Beside the fake reform pretensions of the men who cast him
out, Vare's candor was refreshing. Compared with the hypocrisy
of men who piously talked about repudiating Vareism but who
continued to play the old game for all they were worth—Vare's
own character stands in sharp contrast. Indeed the greatest danger
to progress today is from the pseudo-reformers, the pretended
liberals who seize power only to abuse it as of old. . . . He made
many real friends, many fair weather friends. That the disloyal
as well as the loyal will mourn his passing may be due as much
to shame as to pretense. For while they were with him one day,
against him the next, "regulars" and reformers alternately—Vare
was Vare.[47]

Allegiance and loyalty to one's friends were the cardinal virtues
in Vare's political philosophy. Sitting on the porch of his Berkeley
Square home in Atlantic City among his friends and followers on
Sunday afternoons (it was the surest sign he liked a person or
favored his advancement in politics when he was invited down to
such sessions), he would often remind them that loyalty was what
he expected first of all. An officeholder he had helped, ascending
the porch steps one day, was greeted with the curt remark, "Well,
where have you been? Since you got what you want, you don't
come to see me any more. That's gratitude." With him a political
debt was a debt to be paid and when the debtor was unable or
unwilling to pay, he might be told, as one distinguished Phil-
adelphian, a friend of one of the chief county officers, was told
one day, to "get out, you and your friend are nothing but a pair
of ingrates."[48] Nor did it matter to him how high in political life
his debtor might be. A debt was still a debt. Golder, before his
falling out with Vare, undoubtedly voiced the sentiments of his
leader in 1932 when he declared that the Philadelphia organization did not owe Hoover anything; and recalling in blunt terms
that Hoover did not raise his hand to save Vare, intimated that
there was no real reason why Vare should now save Hoover from

defeat at the hands of the National Republican convention.[49] Nor did it matter to Vare what the effect of such personal loyalty might be upon government or the citizen. In Vare's eyes an office-holder's primary duty was to him and not to the public he was elected to serve. When Monaghan, the district attorney who had failed to save Vare's ward leader, Matt Patterson, from a prison sentence in the grand-jury investigation of 1929 (Vare and his lieutenants saw the investigation as a part of a big plan to destroy Vare), desired to get back into Vare's good graces in 1931, Vare sent him word that he would see him "if you bring Matt Patterson along with you."[50] Because "the Republican organization of Phil-adelphia" had "taken political care of Monaghan since 1896," he should have "taken care" of the organization.[51] It is probably safe to say that the best qualification that an office seeker could present to Vare (or the best argument against dismissal from public office) was loyalty to the Vare leadership. Thus Senator Sam Salus declared for Vare in 1931: "All leaders who stood by Vare when we were in the gloom will be well taken care of."[52]

VI

"Ours is the most perfect party organization in the world. I'll tell you why—it is the greatest welfare organization in the world. It does more to help the poor people. Race, creed and nationality make no difference. It administers to all. It looks after the wants of the poor and the sick." This is one of the first ideas that the boss told me; a minute later he added, "Our Republican organization in Philadelphia is different from Tammany. We won't allow any precinct men to accept presents. We would ostracize him if we knew he accepted gifts of any sort from the people." (Of course many of the organization's finest did accept gifts in silver and gold; but the Philadelphia Republican organization did not employ detectives, nor did it include investigating committees!)

Both in words and in deeds Vare revealed that the basis of the strength of his organization was *personal service*.

"The Philadelphia organization," Vare explained to the Senate committee investigating campaign expenditures in 1926, "is not only founded on republicanism, but one of its cardinal principles is to be of service all along the line from the smallest officer up to the highest who is a candidate. They are instilled with the thought of service—service to their immediate neighbors; and as a result of that, division men are constantly active, not only in the dissemination of information, because they have to very frequently combat opposition stories in newspapers; so that while we are short of having public newspapers to advocate the cause of the Republican organization, we do have an efficient party organization that is constantly in touch with the wants of the people."[53]

Over and over again, Vare emphasized "service." "The Philadelphia organization is successful because it serves the people." And again, "It is the greatest in the country, not alone because it is able to get out the vote, but because it has the confidence of the people, and for nearly two years has been engaged in a vast relief work in every ward."[54]

"These services that the organization does are of various kinds. An immigrant lands in Philadelphia; the party committeeman helps him become adjusted in his new environment. I recall when Jewish people first moved into the first ward. The police wanted to interfere with some of their native practices—we stood between them and the police. Their children might play ball and break a window and the precinct man would go bail for them or get them discharged and see that the broken window was replaced."

One night at the Union Republican Club an old-time politician said to me, "I saw Senator Ed Vare give out a thousand tons of coal in the 1st and 39th wards." A close personal friend of the late Ed Vare told me on another occasion that twenty years before, the average amount that Ed gave daily was $200. "The Vares were always getting their people out of trouble. Ed Vare had a drawer that was like a regular cashier's drawer, with fives, tens, and ones. When a person came for help, Ed would find out about him, and then reach into one of the three compartments and hand the constituent a bill with a smile. I think that the amount of money that they later gave away amounted to more than $6,000 a month. Wm. Vare is generous too—only when Ed was living he was the man that did the charity work, because he had charge of it." (He was the politician; Bill was the contractor.) The money finally came out of the same pocket. An old-time admirer of Vare's wrote to the Pittsburgh *Public Ledger* at the time of the boss's death: "I have known him to do thousands of kindly, charitable and friendly things of which no mention has ever been allowed to reach the types. Only a few weeks ago hc did one of those kindly, generous things for a man long associated with him—a thing which cost him several thousands of dollars. I wanted to write the story. 'Not a word about it,' said Vare. 'It's a personal matter and I want no mention made of it.' "[55]

Pennsylvania provides a number of political scholarships for the schools of higher learning. These scholarships are awarded by the state senators. The Vares have provided enough boys in South Philadelphia and in other sections with free tuition to create a college numbering more students than there are in Swarthmore College. To these students—doctors, dentists, lawyers, and those who have pursued commercial or liberal arts courses—Vare was a benevolent despot whose despotism had not particularly touched them but whose benevolence had made it possible for them to obtain a university education. These university people were a stable section of Vare's political capital. Many of them were active in his organization; all were part of his public. He knew the wisdom of Solomon, "Cast thy bread upon the waters: for thou shalt find it after many days."

Vare was reminded of the gratitude felt by these people in a variety of ways and places. The ballot box was only one of them. Once while crossing the ocean, a young man came over to Vare and introduced himself. "Senator, I am——. I don't know whether you remember me or not. I am practicing law. I am happy to say that I have been fairly successful. I want to thank you for my success, and I am at your service." Vare thanked him and asked how he was responsible for the young man's success. "I'll tell you," said the young lawyer. "I live in South Philadelphia. One year after I entered Pennsylvania Law School I found that the finances had given out and I was unable to finish. So I spoke to some of

my friends, and they said, 'Go over and see the Vares.' I came
to you and you helped me. I want you to know that I appreciate
it." This one testimonial could stand for a thousand. The Vares'
services included scholarships or tuition, as well as silver and
gold for hospital treatment, doctor bills, coal, food, rent, and
relief from nearly every trouble that the flesh is heir to—all the
way from the discharge of a case pending in the magistrate's
court or a comfortable place on the public payroll to a remission
of a $290,000 income tax for an individual, or even more valued
favors to a department store, to the Philadelphia Rapid Transit,
or to the Pennsylvania Railroad or some other utility. One time
an old-line manufacturer paid a $290,000 income tax under pro-
test. Then business got bad; he tried to get the money refunded,
but could not. He went to Vare and said that his financial condition was very bad and that he needed the money. The leader
said that he would see Mellon. Mellon said that it was a good
claim, that the money would come in due course of time. Vare
replied. "Send it now; this is urgent." And Mellon did. I need not
add that this manufacturer's choice at the polls was settled for a
lifetime—he was for Vare. It was also true that the manufacturer's
strength was as the strength of ten—not because his heart was
pure but because he employed men.

Sometimes the services that Vare's organization performed
for the voter in trouble were not strictly legal, as Vare himself
admitted before the Senate investigating committee in 1926. Vare
had been elaborating on what he meant by "service," when Senator Jim Reed, Democrat, Missouri, and the chairman of the
committee, interrupted: "And occasionally getting somebody out
of jail?"

> *Mr. Vare.* I am frank to admit this: I have never called on
> a prohibition enforcement office for assistance. I have never
> called on a district attorney, either Federal or local. I have never
> called on a judge since the Volstead law has been in effect.
> *The Chairman.* I was not talking about that, but this organiza-
> tion—part of its service is to look after fellows who get into trou-
> ble, is it not?
> *Mr. Vare.* We always feel—I say "we." I mean to say that I

believe and many of my friends believe in tempering justice with mercy.

The Chairman. Yes. If a fellow belongs to your crowd, you get him out. That is what you mean, don't you?

Mr. Vare. No. I think we would help most anybody.

Senator King. Is it not a fact—I would not mention this, except that twice you have mentioned this Republican organization was for service—is it not a fact that your Republican organization there has, at times, become so corrupt that there have been revolts among the highminded, patriotic citizens of your city, and they have attempted to overthrow and occasionally have overthrown your machine and tried to give the people a better municipal government? I would not have mentioned that except you have emphasized that twice.[56]

Vare's gifts were the sort that you could see and feel. His official actions in the municipal legislature did much to strengthen his hold on the hearts of his constituents. He represented a section of South Philadelphia in the common council when South Philadelphia received small recognition from that body. The overwhelming majority of its people were either definitely poor or in very modest circumstances. That section had few of the rich men who are always a power in legislation. Vare worked indefatigably for public improvements. This increased his political strength where it counted most. He brought South Philadelphia sewers, manual-training schools, the South Philadelphia High School, the Abigail Vare School. As the former president of the Council told me, "Vare did so many of these things that took millions of dollars that they found out that South Philadelphia had a real live wire who was alive to all the necessities of the section which had formerly been neglected."

Vare's political rise was living proof that power comes, in part at least, from direct service. (As he defined "service" before the investigating committee. "What do I mean by 'service'?" he repeated. "I mean anticipating the needs of a growing community and assisting and cooperating with public developments, the building of schools, the building of children's playgrounds, assisting in hospital work, and all things that go to make up a happy community.")[57]

As a congressman, although he was in a different setting and among his peers rather than his subjects, he was still the same man—as an examination of the *Congressional Record* for the period of 1912-26 reveals. He was still the ward leader—the man who had risen to power on a platform of thousands of personal services. But although his other interests took up a substantial part of his time—so much in fact that he voted on only about 37 per cent of the propositions that came before the House of Representatives and did not make many addresses as compared with the effective congressmen—he did say and vote enough to show where he stood.

He knew that he was in Congress because of the votes he had received in the first Philadelphia district. (On April 4, 1917, he said, "I represent in this House the most stalwart Republican district in this whole country.") He therefore devoted his major efforts to securing the passage of bills of local rather than national importance. His major occupation as a congressman was looking after legislation for his own constituency. He was bent on getting something for his own district—additions to the navy yard, a powder plant, or a new governmental building. He fought valiantly for the continuance of federal governmental functions in Philadelphia, even though the functions had been outworn. The only times he raised his voice concerning matters of national importance were invariably when those matters had to do with the tariff, prohibition (which he opposed), war, or the immigration problem. And although these were national concerns, when Vare spoke on them he spoke with an eye single to Philadelphia, and particularly the first Pennsylvania district.

On the immigration matter he was very explicit. It was his habit to pay many tributes to men of other nationalities and races. In Congress, April 8, 1924, he spoke at length against the bill to limit immigration. His remarks are so descriptive of the politician speaking for his people that I shall quote him in action:

> My observation of the foreigner, and I have had considerable to do with him, both in private life as well as in the execution of great contracts in Philadelphia and places adjacent thereto—I used to pay off on pay day sometimes to the extent of 5,000 persons—

and I never yet had a foreigner of Italian extraction seek more pay than he was entitled to.

In my home in Philadelphia—I virtually have kept open house for the last 30 years, and the people of all classes come there in times of panic and in times of distress, I have had a great many more visitors than in times of prosperity—I want you men from the agriculture sections to know that in all the experience I have had I never have had an Italian immigrant or one of Italian extraction come to my door soliciting alms. I have never had a man or woman of Jewish extraction cither, come and ask for aid, regardless of what the conditions of employment have been. I cannot say that about some of the so-called native Americans.

Philadelphia sees no objection to the immigrant. It takes him and makes a good American out of him. Communities not able to do this should find the wrong in themselves and correct it. The immigrant is educated, and I am proud to say, in a large number of cases, by my political friends. . . .

Vare was one of the few who were farsighted enough to vote against the Volstead law and oppose the 18th Amendment. "When Wilson vetoed the act," he related, "I was one of the minority which voted to sustain his action. My mind was clear at the time of the consequences which would attend the passage of this police legislation and I foresaw long in advance the chaos and general demoralization which would accompany its attempted enforcement."[58] But the real reason why he fought against the prohibition movement is found in a later statement: "In Philadelphia, where my advocacy of the wet cause was pronouncedly popular, my success was assured."[59]

The Philadelphia papers which were fighting "Vareism" often referred to him as a "dependable rubber stamp," who favored all legislation in harmony with "the O-o-old Flag—and a high tariff on Pennsylvania products." And a letter Vare received from President Harding, which he proudly reprinted in his "autobiography," bore out this accusation: "I am sure you can be very useful in the next Congress as you have been in the past and I know full well there will be need of your services."

Vare's prowess in Philadelphia and his influence in the legislative chamber were not only referred to but strongly acknowledged

in more than one congressional debate. To let one example speak
for a number: On February 16, 1926, Vare and Congressman
Welsh (then a ward committeeman in the 24th Ward, later a
Federal district judge) were attempting to get additional funds
for the ill-fated sesquicentennial. Congressman Blanton of Texas
objected:

> Mr. Chairman, it is almost a hopeless task for one to attempt
> to help defeat a bill sponsored by the Vare-Welsh combination.
> I want to compliment our distinguished colleague, for there
> is not in Italy today a dictator with more power in his bailiwick
> than our distinguished colleague from Pennsylvania now exerts in
> his home city of Philadelphia.
> *Mr. Welsh.* Will the gentleman yield?
> *Mr. Blanton.* Not now. The gentleman is one of his lieutenants.
> [*laughter*] But I want to say this: I have been watching and
> noticing my friends, and they have been most amusing. He [Mr.
> Vare] has exhausted the parliamentary rules of this House in an
> attempt to get this resolution appropriating over $4,000,000 at-
> tached to the recent deficiency bill; but he could not do it. But
> when he failed there, through the instrumentality of his colleague
> from Pennsylvania, the old generalissimo of the steering com-
> mittee [Mr. Darrow], he gets a rule brought in to make this
> $4,000,000 proposition. . . .
> *Mr. Berger.* Mr. Chairman, will the gentleman yield?
> *Mr. Blanton.* I do not know how on God's earth they roped
> in the gentleman from Wisconsin, but they have got him.
> [*Laughter*]

A semi-independent in Congress expressed the opinion that
Vare was an astute parliamentarian in Washington. In 1926 he
was ranking member, next but one, to the chairman of the Appropriations Committee. He also quoted Chairman Madden of
the Appropriations Committee as saying that William S. Vare had
one of the greatest funds of factual information of any man on
the Appropriations Committee and spoke particularly of his
marvelously retentive memory.

Vare's organization was not only a service organization—it
was also a *friendly* one. Harry A. Mackey, Vare's campaign
manager in 1926 and leader of the ward, expressed the sentiments
of all of Vare's ward leaders when he said: "If I have got a man

in my ward who does not know every man by his first name who lives in his division, who does not know when that man is in trouble, who does not know when there is want and privation visiting a household—if he knows one man moving out and another comes in and he does not know it, he is no good to me."[60] This was the kind of human, friendly organization that covered the entire city like a finely meshed net. In a few of these meshes the party committeemen were opposed to Vare, but in the overwhelming majority of them they were his personal emissaries. I once met a middle-aged man on a Philadelphia bus as I was returning from Atlantic City. He said that he had about $10,000 worth of property in Philadelphia and that he was against the Vare government because of the high taxes he was forced to pay on his real estate. He lived in the 20th Ward; his party committeeman was Joe Bronson, a real-estate assessor. He liked Joe and said that Joe had done favors for him. "I do not like Vare, but of course, if Joe tells me to vote for Vare, I will." Cases of this sort can be multiplied thousands of times, and thus it was that persons who were opposed to Vare voted for him nonetheless because Vare's party committeeman, whom the voters liked, told them to vote the organization ticket. No one understood more clearly than Vare the value of the little fellows in his organization. For the Vares had learned from personal experience the importance of the little fellows' task. They had once been the most humble of party workers. Bill Vare said he had "learned politics in the practical school of ringing doorbells and holding the check list of voters on election day." George Vare without patronage or funds had successfully fought the Hog Combine in his ward in 1895 because of the wide personal contacts he established. And in running for the first time for state senator, George (like the older La Follette when he ran for district attorney in Dane County, Wisconsin) had made a personal canvass of the entire district. Time after time, in those early years when the Vares were taking over control of the wards of South Philadelphia, the heavy vote which they were able to roll up through the system of personal contacts they were developing swung victory into the Republican ranks for the entire city ticket.

To Vare the division leaders were the vital elements, and he combined them to make the complex compound which was the Republican organization. Moreover, they were elements with insulating properties which, when united, formed a thick impervious layer between the voter's public opinion and his personal affections and interests. Vare himself pointed this out: "Division men are constantly active, not only in the dissemination of information, because they have to very frequently combat opposition stories in newspapers; so that while we are short of having public newspapers to advocate the cause of the Republican organization, we do have an efficient party organization that is constantly in touch with the wants of the people."

Failure of a division leader to bring his division into the Republican column spelled only one thing to Vare: the leader was not on the job day after day, counteracting the poison which a hostile press might instill in the voter's mind against the organization with a thousand friendly acts and services which would bind the voter with ties of gratitude to the organization's representative. To quote again from the testimony of Harry A. Mackey:

Mr. Mackey. . . . but there are 20 wards in Philadelphia where there is no necessity of wasting any material [campaign literature] at all; but to some of the outlaying wards—
Mr. Chairman. What wards did you say?
Mr. Mackey. The first 20. What we call the first 20 wards in Philadelphia are the river wards, and where the foreign population is; and if you ask them the party they will vote for they will name the divison leader.
Senator King. But they vote the Republican ticket?
Mr. Mackey. Absolutely [*laughter*] because the leader is Republican. When they move from one ward to another, and you ask them what ticket they voted in the last division, they will say: "Eddie Green." He happens to be the leader in one division. That is the way they are loyal. . . .
Senator King. What proportion of voters in Philadelphia reside in the wards you just referred to?
Mr. Mackey. About one third.
Senator King. Then one-third of the voters in Philadelphia have no knowledge of American institutions, but just follow their leader?

Mr. Mackey. There are certain ignorant people; we have them out in our residential district. The most ignorant voter in the world is he who thinks he knows how to vote. We have got them out there who wear the high hat and white front; they are too proud to ask how to mark their ballots, and they spoil them every time. [*Laughter*]⁶¹

Later, Mackey strikingly set a concrete price on the division leader—and it was a price that Vare and all the rest of his ward leaders would give their assent to: "We did not give out a dollar more to the Republican city committee when Mr. Vare was a candidate than we would if there had only been the committeemen to elect, because with all due respect to the great office of United States Senator, the Republican organization of Philadelphia can live without a Senator, because we have had that experience a good many years, but it can not live without ward committeemen; and we have almost 3,000 ward committeemen to elect, and that is of the first and vital importance to that organization."⁶²

Vare took many occasions to impress the little fellow with the high regard in which he was held by the "chief." Many of the division leaders Vare knew personally. "Vare politics," wrote a columnist of the *Bulletin,* "always maintained a personal contact with men in the city and county offices. Where other leaders might hold aloof from the little fellows Vare was always ready to meet and greet them. At Christmas when some of the leaders would send gifts to their followers by messenger or by delivery from a store, Vare made the rounds of the offices in the City Hall, calling on the department and bureau heads to extend the greetings of the season to them, but meeting as many of the minor office holders as possible, shaking them by the hand and wishing them a 'Merry Christmas' and frequently leaving a ten or twenty dollar gold piece."⁶³ Vare, it was said, would distribute thousands of dollars at Christmas time to the poor and low-salaried workers throughout the city. "The boys like to be remembered," he was quoted as saying: "They work hard all the year around and deserve consideration. They help me. Why shouldn't I help them?"⁶⁴

"Always, on election day," the *Bulletin* recalled at the time of Vare's death, "no matter what else happened, Bill Vare made the rounds of the divisions in that ward, talking to the boys at the polls, cheering them and boosting the spirit of the organization. In recent years even when crippled and unable to get out of his car, he and Mrs. Vare have made these rounds to show the workers that 'the Senator' as they called him in personal salutation, was with them."[65]

When Vare spoke to an audience of even his humblest political workers, he never addressed them as the Superior One handing down laws from Mount Sinai. There was no condescension in his tone. He possessed the ability to make himself one of them. He became a fellow worker, urging their cooperation. A speech which he made as a ward leader in 1900 to a group of division workers is typical of hundreds of his speeches:

> I have sat here listening to a number of well meaning gentlemen bent upon telling you what to do on election day. It is not my intention to make that kind of a speech. I shan't tell you what to do on election day, because I have a notion that you know better what to do than any of the speakers who have tried to advise you. There isn't any set formula for carrying a division, because each division presents a problem peculiar to itself. The man who lives in a division, knows his people, knows its peculiarities and its problems, is the man best fitted to judge what line of policy is necessary to carry it. If any one were to come to me to try to tell me how to carry my division, I'd be tempted to tell him to save that line of counsel for his own division, and let me go right on using the methods that years of experience with my voters had demonstrated to be best adapted to produce results. You fellows know how to deal with your voters, you know how to talk to them and how to influence them. Nobody can tell you, out of experience in another division of another ward, and among a perhaps entirely different element, how to deal with your people. You know. That's why you are in your ward committee. That's why you are recognized as precinct leaders. All that I am going to ask you to do is what you did last election, and the election which preceded that, and every election—to make your usual house-to-house canvass to see that your voters understand the issues, to see that the other side does not horn in some yarn concocted for the purpose of leading your voters astray. So long as you are on your job, I have no fear that any

emissary of the other side is going to succeed in putting anything over. When a committeeman succumbs before anything of that kind the explanation is not far to seek. He has not been on the job. Now I know that you men are on your job, and that you are going to stay on your job right up to the closing of the polls on election night. And I know you are going to get results, because I know what you can do and I know you will do it. I know that you will keep after your voters until you have lined up every ballot it is humanly possible to get within your precinct boundaries.[66]

Vare's enemies in 1931 tried in vain to explode the legend of Vare's devotion to the little man in politics. On the morning of the magnificent banquet which Vare gave at the Bellevue-Stratford "in honor of the Philadelphia organization," a message was sent on a postcard to the 3,100 division leaders in the city, which was calculated to stir up discontent and resentment against Vare. "Actions speak louder than words. Bill Vare daily gives lip service to the little fellow in politics. He tickles your vanity by telling you that it is because of your service and constant activity that the Republican organization maintains its supremacy. He harps upon friendship, loyalty and devotion to the division man. You produce the votes which make the Vare leadership possible. Wednesday night he is giving a feast to those whom he regards as the real factors in politics. You can readily see what he thinks of you from the fact that you are not invited."[67] But Vare had been too fair in his dealings with the little fellow for this attack to work him any harm.

VII

How much was Vare worth, and how did he get his money? The inventory of William S. Vare on file at the Register of Wills office, City Hall, Philadelphia, shows that he owned $791,000 worth of City of Philadelphia bonds out of a total estate of $1,459,917.24.[68]

During the last years when he was a mere shadow of his former self, it was this wealth more than any other single thing that bound the organization to his leadership. As the leader of the 48th told me, "Dough is politician," and the youngest of the regulars at City Hall knew that a man could not be a leader without a "roll"—without money. Vare explained an early predecessor's success in this way: "I'll tell you why M'Manes was a leader —he was very rich, the president of the bank and a member of the gas trust. He had the right to hire and discharge all employees of the gas works; that, along with his great wealth, gave him his power."

The Vares made their money out of contracts—street-cleaning contracts, paving contracts, contracts for the Pennsylvania Railroad, the Bell Telephone Company, and other utilities. George Vare made the start toward acquiring political power and contracts. One inevitably followed the other. Political power meant contracts, contracts meant money, and money meant increased political power. It was estimated that during the four years 1924-28, the Vare Construction Company was awarded contracts of all kinds amounting to from $15 million to $20 million. A prominent politician who was formerly a lieutenant of Senator Penrose's and later a member of the Vare organization told the following story. At different times he had been with Senator Penrose when the Senator called up the Vares,

> on one occasion Ed Vare and on another occasion Bill Vare, simply saying, "Ed, I need $25,000 immediately." The Senator did not explain why he needed it or where he was to use it, but the money was forthcoming. Sometime later I asked Bill Vare about these rather extraordinary requests, and he said that after he had paid the money, that was the last that he had heard of it. When, however, a question arose between McNichol and the Vares as to who should get certain contracts of the Pennsylvania Railroad and the Bell Telephone Company, Senator Penrose was instrumental in seeing that the Vares were afforded a full share of the contracts. . . . I got the idea that some of this cash was used to persuade certain delegates to state conventions that they ought to recognize the "abilities" of certain candidates as over and above the abilities of candidates not supported by Senator Penrose.[69]

In the spring of 1932 Congressman Golder waged a bitter campaign for renomination in the 4th Congressional District. Vare and the ward leaders in the district were supporting Arthur Sellers, a deputy coroner and the leader of the 32nd Ward, for the Golder place. Golder savagely struck at them over the radio and from the platform. His statements concerning only Vare will be mentioned here. On April 11, 1932, Golder said over WIP:

Yes, this company [the American Telephone and Telegraph Co.] discharged fifty thousand men and women, but the hypocrisy of the situation is shown when you learn that there is one man that they did not discharge. They discharged fifty thousand working men and working women, but they did not discharge their favorite employee, and that man's name is "Vare." Turn to the latest copy of the Bell Telephone Directory of Philadelphia, and there you will find, on the inside of the front cover leaf, the following advertisement:

VARE CONSTRUCTION COMPANY
INCORPORATED
CONTRACTORS AND ENGINEERS
WE CONSTRUCTED
The Bell Telephone Company's
Entire Underground Conduit System

He should have added that this system was constructed on a cost-plus, non-competitive basis, and he should have said that the taxpayers and the stockholders paid the bill.

Mr. Vare, your company's advertisement shows that the Vare Construction Company, Inc., did all the work, but will you tell the people of Philadelphia why you, individually, received from the American Telephone and Telegraph Company: $195,000 in 1925, $265,000 in 1927; over $200,000 in 1928, and why you received from that company in 1929 over $300,000? I challenge you, Mr. Vare, to tell the taxpayers of Philadelphia why you received this money, and how much money you received last year.

On April 1, 1932, over station WCAU, Golder said:

Let me give you one instance of how $40,000,000 was spent to accommodate the Pennsylvania Railroad. The city entered into a contract with the Pennsylvania Railroad for the so-called beautification of the Pennsylvania Railroad. Never was such a contract made between a railroad and a city. The city agreed to pay

The People's Choice

for the beautification of the Pennsylvania Railroad and it was
to spend $89,000,000 of which $40,000,000 have already been
spent. What has been done with this $40,000,000? This
$40,000,000 represents 1/10 of the total indebtedness of the city
of Philadelphia. Let me tell you a few of the things for which
this contract called. The Pennsylvania Railroad owned a property
at 16th and Filbert for which it paid taxes to the city, but which
was of no use to the railroad and they wished to release themselves of the burden of paying taxes. The city accommodated the
Pennsylvania Railroad and paid them $2,000,000 for this ground
which is now being used by the Pennsylvania Railroad, the city
paying for the upkeep and collecting no taxes. The city also
agreed to pay $3,000,000 for the property under the Chinese
wall on Filbert Street and there are no taxes paid on that either.
Atterbury did not like the idea of an elevated over Market Street
in West Philadelphia for it destroyed the beauty of his new
station. Therefore Bill Vare agreed to build a subway out that far
and $26,000,000 of your money is being spent so that the elevated
which serves the people of West Philadelphia shall not interfere
with the beauty of Atterbury's new station.

Why were these things done? Why were policemen discharged?
Why are hospitals closed? The answer is that Bill Vare has the
contracts with the Pennsylvania Railroad and that is just one of
the mediums through which your money travels into the pockets
of Bill Vare. That is why just about the time of that contract
with the Pennsylvania Railroad the books of Bill Vare and his
company showed a mysterious profit of $4,000,000. Later I shall
tell you how the Pennsylvania Railroad created a dummy corporation to handle these deals.

On April 4, 1932, Golder said again over WCAU:

Let me tell you what happened only a few months ago,
through the agency of a dummy corporation, owner of a piece
of ground at 24th and Chestnut Streets. During the last few days
of the Mackey administration, Mackey and his City Solicitor entered into an agreement with the Baltimore and Ohio Railroad and
the owners of this property, whereby it was agreed that $3,900,000
would be paid for part of this property. No one but them knew
of this. $1,900,000 was to be paid by the city to the owners of
this property for so much of the premises as was above the
ground. Did you ever hear of such a bold imposition upon the
public?

I caused an investigation to be made, to determine how much

the owners of this property paid for the property which was being sold to the city at the rate of $3,900,000, and I found according to the certificates upon the deeds, that the people who were selling this property to the city for $3,900,000 paid for it only $750,000. And I say to you: no one else but the City of Philadelphia, no one else but a Vare-controlled gang of grafters would have paid over $400,000 for the untenanted white elephant.

On April 25, 1932, Golder said over WCAU:

I am prepared to prove that in recent years, W. S. Vare received millions upon millions of dollars from the United States Steel, the American Telephone and Telegraph, the Philadelphia Rapid Transit Company, Mitten Management, the Philadelphia Electric and Western Union. And did you know, fellow citizens, that these utilities, the Bell Telephone Company, the Pennsylvania and the Reading Railroads, do not pay any taxes upon their real estate situation in Philadelphia? Oh yes, you pay a tax on your small home, but the Bell Telephone pays no tax upon its millions and millions of dollars of real estate.

Golder was an organization man, or he had been until Vare refused to support him for renomination. It may be assumed that the most devastating attack that can be struck against an institution will always be made by an apostate—particularly if he happens to be intelligent, courageous, and bitter. Congressman Golder was all of these, and in addition he was wealthy. He said what other people in politics believed but did not know. I quote him because the attack so perfectly revealed Vare's ability to "listen and say nothing." For these astounding charges of Congressman Golder brought no response from Vare. He refused to discuss them, and his reply to newspapermen was either "I have nothing to say" or "The big mackerel are biting nicely in Florida now. I caught a dandy." His friends informally discussed the accusations, and said that Golder was an ingrate and a rat to bite the hands that had fed him all these years. Furthermore, Golder was called unkind names and was described as a "fixer" rather than a lawyer, and his clients were described as "racketeers" and "gunmen."

Golder's attack in this campaign against his opponent, a deputy coroner, led to the opponent's arrest and suicide. His attack against the sheriff of Philadelphia, a ward leader in the 4th Congressional District, was the basis of a libel suit in the courts; the sheriff was awarded $5,000 in damages. But Vare never said a word in reply; when the deputy coroner shot himself after he had beaten Golder in the primary, Vare sent a message of condolence to the family, and was quoted in the press as saying, "Art Sellers was my friend—I have known him for thirty years."

As I have said, Vare gained, first because his brothers were successful politicians ahead of him. The three Vares were as close as brothers could possibly be; to Ed Vare, William was always "our Will." Second, he gained because he had great wealth; and no one without wealth could survive as boss of the Philadelphia organization. Although the political boss may be assumed to receive more out of politics than he puts into it, he, or his backers, must be independently wealthy to seize and keep the throne. Here, at the core of things, there was no politics within politics. Gold was king.

As a corollary, the political boss of a great city is usually selected or accepted by the public utilities. Vare was no exception to this custom. He was a contact man between the utilities above and the city committee and voters below. Both the superstructure and the substructure of the boss must be seen before one can understand his place in the Great Society of an American city.

VIII

Vare's victory in the senatorial primary and general election of 1926 marked the climax in his life. Until that time his fortunes had been rising; and at their flood he had achieved his life's ambition—election to a seat in the highest legislative body of the land. With the climax past, however, the denouement was inevitable—despite the fact that, with the realism of life itself, Vare's destruction was to be unwound slowly, in halting measure.

With his fortunes on the ebb tide, Vare proved himself as much a man in adversity as he had been in prosperity—as the account of his last six years will show.

Vare was refused his seat in the United States Senate in 1929, after investigations and delays lasting three years. The Senate's committee concluded that "Vare did receive a plurality of the legal votes" (he had been accused by his Democratic opponent of having permitted all kinds of fraudulent voting at the Philadelphia ballot boxes). The Senate found that "if all the illegal votes were cast out, Vare would still have a plurality . . . but, on account of the excessive expenditure of money in the election itself, and fraud committed by the contestee or by others in his behalf, the contestee's title to the said office is tainted with fraud. . . . We conclude therefore that the contestee is not entitled to a seat in the Senate as a senator from the state of Pennsylvania."

On August 1, 1928, Senator Vare had had a stroke; his collapse was probably caused by the strain of the Senate's prolonged inquiry. For some two months after the stroke his life was despaired of. Physicians thought he would never recover. Newspapermen kept a death watch at his door. Politicians began to prepare plans for a new leadership. But the physicians, politicians, and reporters were wrong. Vare rallied and recovered. The stroke, however, left its mark. He emerged a bent and crippled man, aged beyond his years—but still gripping his most prized possession, his political power, and still determined to fight till the final count for his seat in the senate.

Just before the final decision in 1929, Vare was allowed to plead his own case to the Senate. Senator Norris was at the height of a bitter and prolonged denunciation of the Vare machine, when Vare entered, crippled by paralysis, far from the vigorous man who had first fought for admission to the Senate two years before. The few senators on the floor and the scattered spectators in the galleries were listening without great interest. The door to the side of the presiding officer's stand swung open, and Vare came slowly into the chamber. His face was flushed a wine red, and he walked leaning heavily upon his cane, which he held in his right hand, and upon the arm of Dr. Shaw, who was at his left side, which was crippled.

Up the center of the middle aisle the little group proceeded, with several pages running ahead. Vare looked up and about him. He seemed to be recalling the stirring scenes of two years before, when an earlier round in his long battle was fought. With a little difficulty he lifted himself across the first elevation in the aisle and stood beside the desk of Senator Robinson. The gallery craned forward to watch the stocky man in the dark-brown suit. Senator Norris halted momentarily in his speech. Vare extended the hand in which he had his cane to Senator Robinson, who clasped it with a smile. He then shook hands with Senator McKellar of Tennessee, Senator Johnson of California, and several others who were nearby.

He was led to the seat of Senator Norbeck, South Dakota, which was in the very front row of the chamber on the Republican side. Dr. Shaw took a seat immediately behind. It was obvious that Vare was undergoing a great strain, but it seemed to have little effect upon him. He sat chatting for a moment with Senator Johnson, who was at his right, and then he faced forward stolidly. Vare had many friends scattered in the gallery, but he did not look up. His wife, sitting alone, was directly in the rear of him. In a few moments the dramatic interval ended. Vare sat without moving. The Nebraskan again plunged into his attack upon the political organization of the man who sat before him.

Suddenly Senator David Reed, who as the other Republican senator from Pennsylvania was leading Vare's fight in the Senate, rose and interrupted: "Mr. Vare is here, and has something to say." It was just 12:35 P.M. when Vare began. His voice was harsh and somewhat hesitant. There was a deathly silence in the chamber. Vare read slowly and his words, carefully pronounced, penetrated to the farthest corners. Those who had believed him incapable of the ordeal were amazed at the manner in which he forged slowly through his address. His hand trembled but slightly, although he was forced several times to stop and drink water. The various sheets of his manuscript were handed him by Dr. Shaw. He spoke for twenty minutes. He told the Senate that he had never in all the years he had been in politics stolen an election. He insisted that he had been regularly, legally, and honestly elected senator. He wanted the office, and the Senate would not be playing square if it denied him the place. He was unjustly charged with a grave offense against the laws of the land, a charge that greatly aggrieved him, and which he believed had aggravated his "bodily afflictions."

I never asked anyone to make a false election return such as to change any election records to decide a close contest in my favor. I believe I can truthfully say that the same charge could be brought against everyone elected to public office if the ballots and election records were counted by his political enemies and a report made on their inferences and theories, without any consideration of the proofs of the facts as legal proofs. In fact I am informed by my attorneys who have studied a condensed report of the tabulator of the sub-committee on privileges and elections, furnished by both Wilson (his Democratic opponent who brought the fraud charges) and myself, that the charges are proved to be absolutely false. . . . I challenge any man in the Senate to point to a single bit of evidence of any fraud or conspiracy practiced by myself or by any of my friends in the three-cornered primary when I won the Republican nomination from the former Senator Pepper and the then Governor Pinchot. . . . Not one voice was raised against that primary in Pennsylvania until the question of expenditures was brought in as an issue.

"Am I to be condemned because without a newspaper, with the State organization and the county organization against me and my friends, we were compelled to spend one-third of what our principal opponents spent in bringing the issues of the campaign to the 4,000,000 voters of the State? . . . In the Pennsylvania campaign the expenditures now charged to me alone instead of all the candidates banded with me, were $1.30 per vote, $81.75 per thousand of population and $91.68 per voting district. Those of the Pepper-Fisher state ticket were $3.50 per vote, $187.74 per thousand population, and $210.59 per voting district. There were 1,451,557 votes cast in that primary, and the expenditure of my ticket represented 54 cents per vote. . . . In Nevada the cost per vote cast in the last election was $4.46, and in Montana, $2.57, and such costs were even greater in New York. Also the Republican expenditures of 24 states and Democratic expenditures in 19 states in the last election were greater per capita than that of the election in which I was elected." Sitting down he drank a glass of water and was handed some medicine by Dr. Shaw. He left the Senate chamber slowly but without outward sign of the strain he must have sustained.[70]

Vare, in the same brown suit he had worn when he pleaded his case, was present again when the vote was taken which barred him from the Senate forever. When Vare entered, Senator Pittman, Democrat, Nevada, was charging that his election had been tainted with fraud. Vare did not look around at the speaker, who was a few feet to his left. "Five minutes after twelve Vare will not be a contestant for this seat!" shouted Pittman. Vare looked stolidly ahead and scratched his chin with his able hand. The vote was but five minutes away. He was like a man already defeated. "Fraud, fraud, fraud" was being dinned into his ears by Pittman. Pittman ended, and Wheeler, Democrat, Montana, rose and declared "We all know that in a minute we're going to say to Vare, 'You stole the election.' "Vare looked dully at Wheeler. The clock pointed to noon, and Curtis rapped for order. Norris rose and moved the question. The clerk read the resolution. There was a murmur in the crowded gallery. Vare sat with an inscrutable expression upon his face, now a deep red. In the gallery his wife and two daughters leaned forward nervously. The roll call followed. As the clerk proceeded through the list of names Vare did not change expression, although early in the count it was apparent that his long struggle was quickly passing into the shadow of defeat. Senator Reed, who had led the long Vare fight on the floor, sat with his head resting upon one hand, apparently more dejected than Vare himself. The call of the roll was finished; Vare was through. He talked one instant with Dr. Shaw and then hobbled slowly down the center aisle and out of the Senate forever. His face was set; he looked like a man crushed by a great blow. In the gallery his wife and two daughters sat, not weeping but staring ahead fixedly. However, a few minutes later Beatrice Vare began to weep softly.

The crushing defeat of the Philadelphia leader amazed even those of his followers who had sat through the fight. Only the core of the Republican Old Guard had stuck by him. Desertions from the right wing in the chamber and the irresistible force of the Democratic-Insurgent coalition made the contest so one-sided that the vote was 58 to 22.[71]

Vare's supporters had justified their huge campaign expenditures by pointing out that the money was not spent for Vare alone but was used to elect a slate of 5,000 candidates besides Vare. "There were 35 Republican state senators to be nominated; there were 36 Republican congressmen to be nominated; there were 208 members of the lower house of the state legislature to be nominated; there were 113 members of the Republican state committee to be selected. In addition to that there were county chairmen in each of the counties, and in each of the counties were the precinct representatives, who under the Pennsylvania laws, are elected by the people of their respective counties."[72] Vare claimed as his own personal expenses only the $71,435 spent in his letter-writing campaign.

Other costs included those for newspaper advertising, amounting to $61,728 for advertisements in 168 English-speaking and 77 foreign-language papers. The 475,000 specimen ballots cost 6.5 cents each, or $27,625. Other expenditures were for the 8,590,000 pieces of literature mailed out, the posting of bills, souvenir booklets, programs, books, special editions of various newspapers, preparation of literature, the paying of speakers to acquaint the electorate with the platform, office payrolls running as high as $8,000 a week in Pittsburgh, multigraphing volumes of materials, telegraph and telephone charges, badges, speaker cars, and meals.

Even incidental expenses around a campaign headquarters ran high, as shown by those in Pittsburgh. To give the place a carnival atmosphere cost $400; bill posting in Pittsburgh totaled $4,800; to have a band on hand ran to $994; $500 was spent in soliciting workers from door to door. Automobiles were rented for $1,435 to carry speakers to meetings; special banquets cost $160.[73]

The expense which drew the greatest fire of attack, however, was the money spent on hiring watchers. According to the Pennsylvania primary law passed in 1906, the hiring of watchers was a perfectly legal act. These watchers were at the polls throughout election day looking after the interests of their candidate and seeing that he was fairly represented and that all ballots cast for him were counted. Such watchers were paid ten dollars a day for their services. In Pittsburgh, Pepper had 35,000 watchers and Vare 14,000.[74]

The exact number of watchers used by Vare could not be estimated because of Mackey's peculiar interpretation of the term: "Of course a watcher is to watch, but if he has not got any voters going to the polls to watch he has got nothing to watch. It is his duty to go out and see that the voters come in; then he can watch them as long as he pleases. Therefore, a watcher to me is a worker, a man who goes and gets out the votes."[75]

The Philadelphia organization always paid out at least fifty dollars to a division, and let the division leader pay out the money to as many workers as he could get, not all of them holding watcher's certificates, but serving as watchers just the same.[76] Thus a gang of hoodlums could pack a polling place and yet all be labeled as watchers.

But despite such well-marshaled arguments, Vare was refused his seat by a Senate twenty of whose members' per capita expenditures in the campaign the year before had exceeded Vare's.[77]

But Vare was faced with a barrier of adverse public opinion— an opinion that had been only too well expressed in that 1926 senatorial primary when he was bitterly and strenuously opposed by the Philadelphia newspapers as well as by those in other sections of the state. After his victory in the primary, these Philadelphia newspapers, with the exception of the *Record,* turned about and favored Vare for the election. The *Record,* the one liberal newspaper in Philadelphia, campaigned for Vare's opponent, Wilson, by reprinting statements that Republican newspapers and leaders had made against their candidate in the primary campaign. On May 11, the *Evening Bulletin* published a statement on Vare which the *Record* reprinted in a special box on its front page of October 25, 1926. The statement follows:

> A vote for Congressman Vare would be a vote for the exaltation of the Vare system of politics, registration list padding, ballot-box stuffing, tally sheet manipulation, public office pay, to the dignity of the Senatorial toga. The record of the Vare machine

is written, sworn to by witnesses in court, passed by judge and jury. The substitution of Congressman Vare for Senator Pepper would be an announcement to the nation that the state of Pennsylvania puts the method of the ward politicians and this political machinery above the capability of statecraft.

The Pittsburgh *Public Ledger* on May 17 of the same year, and the Philadelphia *Record* on October 19, carried this statement:

Vare is a local ward boss, who by fair means or foul has extended his control over the political machine of the entire city. He is a typical product of the lowest form of American politics. He rules by arbitrary forces, not by ability and politics and character or by his personal hold upon the loyalty of his workmen. His machine is indelibly branded by its habitual resort to trickery and fraud in its conduct of elections. The epithet of "Sticker Bill" has been fastened upon him by his treachery to a friend whom he tried to defeat on his death-bed lest the office for which he was a candidate should pass from the Vare control. Vare's ambition to make himself a Senator would be ludicrous were not the menace of his winning a serious one.

The *Record* on October 29 rescued from oblivion this statement which the *Inquirer* had originally published on April 14:

Mr. Vare is of, by, and for the political machine which he dominates. He is a machine-made man—a product of its methods. He is not of Senatorial timber. His training is not for statesmanship. His familiarity is not with grave public questions, but with the trade of tricky policies and the men who are adept in all sorts of election corruption. He would not be welcomed into the Senate. He would be lost there, and the state would be humilitated by his presence.

On May 17 the *Evening Public Ledger* published a statement that the *Record* featured on October 9:

No one who knows him [Vare] thinks he is of Senatorial size. He began as a ward politician and, although other men who began in that way have developed qualities of leadership, Mr. Vare has remained a ward politician, with a ward politician's narrowness of mind and ignorance of the broad principles of government.

The *Record* on October 12 republished a remark that Senator Pepper had made on March 17. I might add that no attack in the campaign angered the Vare men so much, or did Pepper so much harm, as did this one.

> This fight gives the Philadelphia organization a first-class chance to throw Vare overboard. He is the Jonah of the organization. . . . When at Washington and through the country people are skeptical about the Sesqui-Centennial because they believe the Mayor's best efforts are being hampered by Vare, it will be fine to be able to assure them that we are going to celebrate our independence by pitching Vare into the river. Philadelphia has not had such a chance since we did a similar trick 150 years ago.

However, in 1930, Senator Pepper, in his book *In the Senate,*[78] sanely observed, in commenting on the primary in which he was defeated:

> Naturally there was talk of trading, of defections within the ranks and of election-booth irregularities. There were, in others words, the veiled charges of the type that follow every bitterly contested primary fight. Personally I saw no definite proof that these charges were true to any such extent as to change the result of the primary. I accordingly followed the maxim familiar to lawyers, that your first duty is to take your licking like a gentleman. Pinchot, however, brought the charges prominently into the light when, in his official communication as governor, certifying to the Senate the later election of Vare, he made the assertion that the nomination was "partly bought and partly stolen."

It is doubtless safe to say that Vare was disposed of without regard to the evidence unearthed by the committee, and that he would have been denied a seat in spite of the evidence; it is also safe to say that had Senator Pepper won in the election, spending twice the amount Vare did, and benefiting by the same and usual tactics and practices at the ballot box, the probability is that his right to a seat would never have been seriously questioned. The Senate refused Vare admission, not for any illegal act but for general reasons similar to those that closed the portals of the

Union League to him—he was a ward politician without social background.

The municipal election of 1927 had been a smashing victory for Vare. His hand-picked candidates were swept into office with large majorities. His machine was a perfectly attuned as ever. He was riding the height of his political power. But his triumph was short-lived. For ever after his stroke in August of 1928, there was a cloud of uncertainty hanging over his leadership. Thenceforth he was a sick man, and often so seriously weak that he lacked the personal strength necessary to take the field in political battles, whether to lead his friends or to oppose his enemies, who were not slow in appearing on the scene.

Largely in the hands of the men about him, the situation was ideal for the appearance of a Cardinal Wolsey. The traitor appeared in the form of the brilliant and astute Harry Arista Mackey. As a reward for managing his campaign in 1926, Vare had made him mayor in 1927. Congressman Ransley and other politicians predicted that he would be treacherous, but Vare took a chance. "He served me—I can do no more now than serve him."

During the same August that he was stricken, a grand-jury investigation had been started. It was called ostensibly to investigate racketeering in Philadelphia; there had been a murder of a notorious character, and there were rumors of police and political protection. The jurors uncovered much evidence of an alliance between crime and the police and certain politicians. A searching inquiry into governmental affairs in a great city like New York, Chicago, or Philadelphia is likely to uncover something at any time, and August, 1928, was no exception. This grand-jury investigation, like many other reform movements, served a dual purpose. As it progressed during Senator Vare's illness it was used as a weapon to strike at him. Mayor Mackey and District Attorney Monaghan (long a Vare stalwart), George Holmes (a county commissioner and one of Vare's right-hand men), and later Albert Greenfield (who described himself in 1926 as the largest property holder in Philadelphia, and who raised much of the acknowledged expenditures of $785,964 in the Vare campaign and admitted personal contributions of $125,000 to Vare's war chest in 1926)—these four Vare men decided that since Vare was about to die, somebody would have to take over the leadership—an opportunity of a lifetime!—and they reached for it.

They tried to get other key men friendly to Vare, and in some cases failed, as in the case of Judge Leopold Glass. (Judge Glass was at that time president judge of the Municipal Court. There was much patronage connected with the court—five or six hundred places. They thought that with Judge Glass they could control these places; they also wanted the Judge because of the moral support it would give them. He was as close to Vare as a son. He was told that he would be a great leader in the new order— "As it is, I understand you haven't enough votes [among the judges] to get yourself re-elected [as president judge]. Leopold, if you seek my help I will gladly give it." But Judge Glass stood firm. He said, "I wouldn't desert Vare, and especially now that he is sick!" (It cost him the president judgeship.)

One ward leader, a Vare man, was sent to jail; but what riveted the attention of the organization was the forced resignation of the affable Harry C. Davis from his place as director of public safety. He had originally been placed there at the suggestion of Vare. He was the director of the City Committee, and Vare's detail man and friend. As one singularly astute politician saw it, "matters went from bad to worse, and gradually every one of the ward leaders [through District Attorney Monaghan's office] that they 'had something on' were whipped into line, numbering together about fifteen. At this point the old organization stand-bys began to rally, led by Harry J. Trainer, Tom Cunningham, Charlie Hall, Billy Campbell, and Sam Salus."

By the beginning of 1929 nearly half the police force had been either discharged or transferred or demoted. The investigation lost momentum, however, when it struck the trial of three powerful gamblers, one of whom was undisputed master of a ward and was reputed to be closely connected with the district attorney's office; for good and substantial reasons it would have been unwise to seriously prosecute this trio.

The City Council, with the exception of Mackey's man, Councilman Levick, remained loyal to Vare, and so did the Civil Service Commission. Those opposed to Vare attempted to take the power over the police away from the commission and to give it to the director of public safety, but Senator Salus was able to prevent this change from being made at Harrisburg.

The battle line was drawn in the municipal election of 1929, in which the powerful "row" offices were to be filled, including city treasurer, city controller, register of wills, and coroner. Thomas Raeburn White, a lifelong reformer, organized the Republican League with the hope of electing reform candidates to the row offices. Mackey, who had in the meantime become associated with Greenfield, planned to place his man, John Dugan, in the city treasurer's office. Johnnie Dugan became one of the most popular of all the ward leaders; he was at that time director of public welfare. Mackey's idea was to bring Dugan out for register of wills against Billy Campbell. The Vare organization would support Campbell, but might possibly compromise on Dugan for city treasurer as a harmony move. The idea was to put the post of city treasurer into the hands of someone who would work with wealthy real-estate operator Greenfield. This plan failed; Vare issued a statement, "No compromise with Mackey."

Mackey then started to organize his own support and with the help of District Attorney Monaghan tried to round up ward leaders. He was not very successful with this, and he joined forces with the Republican League. Vare shrewdly took the fire out of the League's appeal by endorsing William B. Hadley, a person of ability and honesty and with no political connections, for city controller. This strategic move won the battle for Vare. The honest-to-goodness reformers and Mackey and his friends made a poor showing at the polls.

Vare himself was seemingly ill unto death at Atlantic City. He was unable to do any campaigning, but the Vare institution never faltered. In spite of Dugan's popularity he was overwhelmingly defeated for the office of register of wills, by a majority of 153,000; the other Republican League (Mackey *et al.*) candidates went down to defeat by more than 200,000. Thus even

though the leader was absent, he had enough loyal and active
lieutenants in the field to carry his ticket to large victorious majorities. The first move to take Vare's toga had failed.

Al Smith had given the Vare organization a real jolt, too, in
1928. The "Al" idea was so appealing to the people in Vare's
home ward, the first, that its leader, who was Vare's personal
representative, failed to keep it in the Republican column. The
contest in this bailiwick was particularly significant as an instance when popular opinion, largely unorganized, defeated a
candidate supported by an overwhelming majority of the newspapers and one of the best ward organizations in the city. Furthermore, the Al Smith leader of the ward in this fight was a fake, for
in reality he was one of the Republican division leaders who
played a Democratic role for this specific occasion. He took
charge of the Democratic campaign because the ward boss thought
that "it would be better to have me leading this movement than
an outsider." Yet the Democrats won. They "swept over us like a
wave." Four other wards in this original Vare stronghold were
carried by the Democrats. Even more damaging to Vare's prestige
was the defeat of the widow of his brother, Edwin, Flora M.
Vare, who had been holding the senate seat that he and his brother
George had held since 1896. Her defeat was the result, in part at
least, of faulty campaign tactics. Al Smith got under the skin of
the people in South Philadelphia. Some of these people told their
leaders that if they could vote for Al they would give the organization the rest of the ticket. These division leaders were badly
advised. They replied that the vote must be for Hoover or nothing. In too many cases, at least for Senator Flora Vare, it was
nothing. The loss of Vare wards from the Hoover column and of
Flora Vare's senate seat in the same district showed some people
that Vare's organization could be beaten, and that in the very
core of Vareville!

During the years after the momentous Senate decision and the
stroke, Vare made a superb fight to keep control of his own
organization. In the face of inevitable physical weakness he carried
on to the limit of his powers. During that summer of 1930 he
would still come to his office in the Land Title Building in Phil-

adelphia several times a week. His Negro chauffeur, Oliver, would drive him there in his big Packard. He would usually arrive about noon, remain for an hour or two, sometimes less. He would go into his office—its outer door lettered "Vare Construction Company"—and find Harry Snow, his secretary, and Mrs. Knight, his stenographer, present. There would also be from three to seven ward leaders or other citizens there to see the Big Fellow. The politicians made this outer office a little city hall. Their talks were so interesting that I always forgot that I was waiting.

I know of at least one instance since his great illness when he definitely asserted his mastery over a man who had wanted to think of the leader in the past tense. Vare had asked his secretary to phone and ask a member of the mayor's cabinet at City Hall to see him at once. This certain director was rather curt, and sent back a message saying that he would be there later. When the Senator received this reply to his order, he came to the door of the outer office, drew himself up, and with a hard, flintlike expression, said, "Tell him that I shall expect to see him in my office in fifteen minutes." The man was there in less than fifteen minutes. The office group observed this incident with great satisfaction; to them it indicated that all was well with Philadelphia —that the boss's word was still law.

After he had entered his office, on the days when he drove up from his Atlantic City home, someone of those present would go in to see the Senator, and be there from ten minutes to an hour. Whenever the leader passed through the outer room, talking ceased; everyone stood obsequiously at attention. Sometimes he would leave before everyone had had an opportunity to go in. A given person might then press forward and whisper into the Senator's ear the nature of his difficulty. The expression on Vare's face never changed. He would listen and then either say that he could do nothing, or turn toward Harry Snow and give him a few words of instruction. As one of his associates has put it, "His ability to dovetail the ambitions of men, and to smooth out the misunderstandings that naturally arise in political matters, has been really remarkable. I never met a man who devoted more time to the ordinary details of political life than he." Vare held his political scions without the aid of formal conferences. Ill as he was in February of 1932, while he waited at the station for the train that was to take him to Florida, he held conferences with his political followers in the baggage room of the station. During the hour's wait for the Miamian, a steady stream of visitors went in and out of the baggage room to have a few words of conversation with the leader, while those awaiting admittance stamped their feet to keep warm in the brisk air of the platform outside.[79] Vare had just outspokenly endorsed the wet stand of U.S. Senator James J. Davis, and those huddles he held with one follower after another, short though they were, were sufficient to tell his lieutenants exactly what the boss wanted done in the coming primary campaign.

Gradually the leader became weaker and came less and less often to the city or his office. He registered and voted, attended several banquets and meetings, but for the rest of the time was in his home on the boardwalk, or at St. Lucie, Florida.

When he entered the banquet given to Ed Kelly urging Kelly's nomination for the office of district attorney, all the guests cheered. Senator Vare took his place near the center of the long speakers' table. There were many speeches that night; his was much the shortest, and it was given with difficulty. All I heard was the words "I am a friend of Ed Kelly's" (his counsel in the Senate investigation of 1926-29) and "I am happy to be here." Later there was a fetching dance done by a little girl, on the platform behind Vare and J. Hampton Moore, who was sitting nearby. The Senator turned to observe the dance, but the ascetic-looking Mr. Moore looked straight ahead without blinking an eyelash. Vare left the banquet before it was ended. As he passed down the side of the room a seasoned ward leader, the coroner of Philadelphia, seized his hand and bowed so low over it that I was surprised at his agility. If this great homage from the leader of the 45th Ward made an impression on Vare, he gave no sign of it. He was helped onto the elevator as quickly as his eager friends would permit.

Vare, in 1931, gave a dinner for the Philadelphia Republican organization at the Bellevue-Stratford Hotel which, it was rumored, cost him $10,000. Among the five hundred guests present were three United States senators, the entire congressional delegation from Philadelphia, a state supreme court justice, twenty-two judges of the courts of his home county, many state senators, and a score of assemblymen. More emaciated than at any time since the stroke of paralysis that left one side of his body helpless, but of good color and extremely mentally alert, Vare sat in his chair, his face glowing with pride," said the Philadelphia *Record,* in commenting on the banquet. "Nominally leader, but placing his faith in the ability of the now famous War Board to carry out the details of the organization that he and his brothers had helped to build, Vare was a strangely pathetic figure as he gazed out over the crowded ballroom. . . . What it [the dinner] actually demonstrated was the fact that the Republican machine in this city is bigger than Vare and that his control is more nominal than actual. Vare was given plenty of tribute. Many excellent things were said of him, but they were less impressive than the recognition given to the great organization that he helped to create and develop."[80]

In May, 1932, there was a meeting of the state committee at the Bellevue-Stratford Hotel. Not only the city's finest, but also the best politicians of the state were present. Again many prominent politicians were called upon to make speeches. Vare was sitting in the center of the first balcony, directly in front of the stage. When he was called upon, there was marked applause; he painfully rose to his feet, said that he was happy to be present, and sat down. A few minutes later he was helped out of the ballroom, and, assisted by members of his family, he retired to a nearby room. Before he climbed the short flight of stairs, an old-time ward leader pressed forward to touch the Senator's hand. There were others standing in reverential awe who would have done likewise, but Vare was taken away.

But despite Vare's heroic effort to remain the real head of his machine, the best he could do was to provide his organization with absentee leadership, and this was the equivalent of no leadership at all. Just as when an old feudal king, who in strength of his prime had consolidated the holdings of warring barons into a strong kingdom, became so enfeebled that he could no longer rule with the hand of iron and had no heir apparent capable of dominating his powerful lords, so Vare's political barons, unruly still for all the disciplining he had given them, began banding together with an eye to their future advantage in a new regime when the old leader had fallen. Only a few remained faithful to the old king. Some were forming intrigues to reach for the throne itself; others, by means of alliances, were trying to protect their own baronies from the possible ravages of the new king when he appeared. Thus in January, 1932, the Philadelphia *Record* saw six major alliances among Vare's most powerful followers: "What is known as the Hazlett-Cox combination takes in most of the strongly Vare ward leaders; then there is the Trainer-Salus group, also Vare, but refusing to take orders from Hazlett; and the Campbell bloc, which is suspicious of everything in South Philadelphia; also the Weglein-McCaughn band, which is holding the old Cunningham units; not forgetting the Mackey-Dugan tie-up, in step, for the time being, with Vare; finally the Hamilton-Shields organization, strongly Pinchot and fighting for a toe-hold. . . . Other leaderships cut across these lines. For instance, John R. K. Scott, Alfred M. Waldron, Arthur T. Sellers, John J. McKinley, Jr., George Connel, George Deal, David T. Hart, Oscar E. Noll and one or two more are more or less free agents, and are concentrating earnestly upon their own political fences." In the *Record* opinion, "ward leaders right now are seeking to bulwark themselves and their followers against the day when Vare passes from the scene. They are all loyal to Vare, save one, but self-interest is dictating their actions."

"Leaders are born, not made," Vare told me once, as we talked, and then continued, "Some men never acquire leadership. It is easy to be misunderstood. One must have careful advisers. One difficulty is that one set of men try to find out what I want and tell that this is the thing to do; but when I ask a person for his opinion, I want his own opinion. The thing to do is to touch the pulse of the people. I send for people who are not leaders to tell me what the people are thinking about."

This question of advisers—a problem of paramount importance

to all real leaders at any time—became perhaps the most vulnerable factor in the Vare leadership. Senator La Follette's most valued adviser was his wife, but Mrs. Vare had never been interested in politics; she was a good wife, but unfortunately she was no source of political guidance. But Vare's daughter, Beatrice, had the political skill and sense of her father, and after his illness she became increasingly active in politics. She was often present in conferences at their home and spoke in some campaigns. In 1932 she stood like a stone wall against her father's passively endorsing Mackey in his campaign for the state assembly. After James Hazlett, Vare's chairman of the Central Campaign Committee, had endorsed Mackey, Beatrice Vare, mindful of Mackey's treason in 1929, announced that Senator Vare was strongly opposed to Mr. Mackey and that he would ask his friends to support Commissioner Long for the legislature. Miss Vare spoke at a political rally in the 46th Ward, Mackey's own ward; and Mackey was defeated. Old politicians at City Hall spoke of Beatrice (she was then about twenty-six), and sighed, "If she were a boy, what a honey of a politician we would have."

During his last years, in seeking advice concerning the ever-changing political scene, he called on those who he believed were faithful to him. This meant, in many important instances, the sacrifice of talent for loyalty, thereby creating a situation that was a perpetual invitation for intrigue and revolt. Ward leaders who had been lieutenants of the late Boies Penrose, as well as certain Vare stalwarts, were ever on the *qui vive* to seize control.

In 1931, the canny Bill Campbell, three times register of wills and an old Penrose lieutenant, fought Vare's men for council in the northeastern part of the city. The Campbell group (Campbell, Crossman, McKinley, and Daly) won against Jimmie Clark, Coroner Schwartz, and Real Estate Assessor (later Mercantile Appraiser) Dave Hart. Campbell raised the cry "Home Rule for the northeast—no more domination from South Philadelphia!"— but the controlling factor in this councilmanic campaign was the fact that the leaders in four wards with 330 committeemen fought the Vare leaders in three wards with only 170 committeemen. This was an instance in which Vare was badly advised; all observers conceded his defeat before the primary except Mr. Clark, who advised him. Clark's great virtue was his undying zeal and loyalty in serving Vare; it was regrettable that his ability was so limited.

One can best understand the politicians' state of mind, in 1931, for example, by imagining a pack of forty eight wolves following a wounded leader. The leader is no longer able to run at the head of the pack, but he has a psychic advantage over all pretenders because of past victories; and furthermore, when one or more wolves close in to finish off the leader, they are fought by other members of the pack, because of either fear of what the old leader might do, or loyalty to him, or uncertainty as to their place under the leadership of the wolves that kill the old one. Thus in 1928, Harry J. Trainer, Tom Cunningham, Charlie Hall, and Billy Campbell fought off Mackey when he attempted to make a finish of Vare. And in 1931, when Charlie Hall and Big Tom Cunningham reached for the leadership and Billy Campbell fought Vare in the Northeast, the Trainers again, along with Sam Salus, rallied to the Vare standard. Yet it was the Trainer combine which finally finished Vare off in 1934. The leader survived as long as he did, not because he was strong or because his opponents were weak; his name continued powerful because elections were still being won (despite the jolt Al Smith gave the organization in 1928), and the usurpers could not concentrate on one individual with sufficient power to defeat him.

However, Vare's downfall was nearly encompassed in the pre-primary mayoralty campaign of 1931. At that time Charlie Hall was president of the City Council; he was a former Penrose lieutenant and a foe of Vare's; he was also one of the three or four most powerful politicians in Philadelphia, the right-hand man of the Pennsylvania Railroad, and a millionaire. For more than a decade he had been leader of the 7th Ward—the home ward of Iz Durham; and before Iz Durham the ward had been led by John M'Manes of the old Gas Trust. Months before the primary, Councilman Hall had been secretly at work lining up the ward leaders for his (and the Pennsylvania Railroad's) candidate for mayor. Hall's plan might have succeeded had he picked a less vulnerable candidate than George H. Biles, who was identified with the Pennslyvania Railroad and political contractors. In spite of this, thirty-two or more of the forty-eight ward leaders had been persuaded to sign on the "dotted line" (a Vare custom) for Biles. However, among the leaders who refused to go along with Hall was the shrewd and powerful Senator Sam Salus, who was absolute master of the 4th Ward. When Charles Hall was most ardently trying to thrust his bare bodkin into the fallen leader's back in the form of the Biles candidacy for mayor, Senator Salus called on Elisha Lee, vice president of the Pennsylvania Railroad. The meeting was rough, and according to City Hall gossip at the time, the Senator slapped Mr. Lee's face and told him to keep his snoot out of Philadelphia politics. Furthermore, he threatened to support Pinchot's program for more adequate utility regulation in the legislature if the railroad crowd continued to support Biles' candidacy. Whether the slap was literal or figurative, the railroad influence diminished.[81]

When Vare, although flat on his back at the time, was asked to go along for Biles, he said that he would spend every cent he had rather than see the contractor's candidate nominated. "Anyone but Biles!" he added. He took the long, lean ascetic-looking independent, J. Hampton Moore, a former foe, and in forty-eight hours the Biles boom had collapsed. The terrific tension of trying to upset a throne killed the powerful Big Tom Cunningham, sheriff of Philadelphia, a few days later; he collapsed talking to Vare on the front porch of the Atlantic City home, which was as seasoned with political talk as any nook or office in City Hall. Charlie Hall was stricken a few days later at the Saratoga race track in New York State. Hall was doomed to political extinction when Biles resigned from the campaign. His "signers" scurried back to Vare. Harry Juenzel, a county commissioner and a lesser political leader, also died at about this time, and it was the opinion of members of his political family that his death was caused by the strain of making the formidable threat against Vare's supremacy.

In addition to the ward leaders who died waiting for Vare to die, there were other casualties of a political sort. Men who guessed wrong about Vare's dying or his strength were deposed as

a result. George Holmes, one of the plotters, had been county commissioner, but he was not "reappointed"; the voters ratified Vare's
choice of a faithful man—the Honorable Jimmie Clark—at the
election. The same thing happened to Harry W. Keely, receiver of
taxes and then Judge Brown's man on the City Committee from
the 15th; a Vare dependable, Arthur Brenner became receiver of
taxes. In those days, one lounging about City Hall and talking to
the regulars there would necessarily have been impressed with
the amount of speculation on Vare's death. It was the substratum
of many conversations—so many that one was constantly reminded of those lines from *King Richard II,* "For God's sake let
us sit upon the ground and tell sad stories of the death of kings."

In the 1932 campaign Vare struck again at those who had
attempted to depose him. For example, he refused to support
Congressman Benjamin Golder, a protégé of former Sheriff
Cunningham, for Congress. Golder thereupon waged a bitter
campaign for renomination in the 4th Congressional District.
Vare and the ward leaders in the district were supporting Arthur
Sellers, a deputy coroner and the leader of the 32nd Ward, for
the Golder place. Golder savagely struck at them over the radio
and from the platform. Golder also charged Vare, citing chapter
and verse, with having received hundreds of thousands of dollars
from the American Telephone and Telegraph Company and the
Pennsylvania Railroad in exchange for Vare's political influence.
Golder was a most effective campaigner and his attacks on the
Vare organization made him even more feared than hated. Yet
Philadelphia went Republican in 1932 by a 70,816 majority.

A series of political accidents in Pennsylvania in 1932 united
to give Vare a wide-open opportunity at the leadership of the
state Republican party. But he was no longer capable of grasping
the prize he had so long sought and had so nearly won in 1926.
While he still had control of his own organization, in Pittsburgh
the *Public Ledger* reported, "the leadership has been split wide
open. Mayor Kline of that city [Philadelphia] is to be tried in
about two weeks for alleged misconduct in office. His political
strength has disappeared and the Republican party in Allegheny
county has split into so many factions that there will be a bitter fight

for control in practically every ward in Pittsburgh at the primaries. The fight there has become such a free-for-all that more than 300 candidates are circulating petitions for the state legislature, although there are only 26 places to be filled from the county. With Governor Pinchot and the state organization at each other's throats in the rest of the state, the solid block of Philadelphia votes has become the balance of power in the state. The Pinchot group and the state organization leaders courted Vare zealously for his support in the state fight. He allied himself with state chairman Martin, at the price of being allowed to dictate the ticket."[82] But Varc's great chance came too late. Unable to keep order in his own domain, he did not have the capacity to win power outside his boundaries.

In the revolution of November 7, 1933, Philadelphia went Democratic in the municipal election by 84,000 votes. And the significance of this Democratic victory must be noted in some detail, for it revealed Vare as a mere mortal who had made grievous mistakes of judgment in the campaign. This defeat powerfully aided his enemies, who decisively defeated him in 1934, just two months before his death on August 7. The organization's defeat in 1933 was caused by the Great Depression, the popularity of Franklin D. Roosevelt, the resentment of the voters toward existing organizations and leaders, and a certain weakness in Vare's leadership.

And it is the last of these factors that will be commented on here. After 1928, as I have said, Philadelphia was governed by absentee leadership—and absentee leadership, like absentee landlordism, is resented by the American people. Vare could no longer keep his finger on the pulse of Philadelphia while he was seriously ill or convalescing in Atlantic City or St. Lucie, Florida. After the warning registered in the September, 1933, primary, however, he took the field in person (from a bed) and moved to the Warwick Hotel in Philadelphia. This might have helped more were brain as keen as it once had been; but it was not. His hand now trembled as he felt the public's pulse; his feel for the drift of public sentiment was no longer sure; his knowledge of the strength and temper of men was inadequate and often inaccurate. All who observed Vare in those last three years could not fail to note how feeble, both mentally and physically, he had grown.

On May 14, 1932, he presided at a meeting of the Pennsylvania delegation. He leaned heavily on General Martin, the chairman of the Republican state committee, who prompted him in nearly everything he said. Before he could state some of the questions, he would have to turn to Martin. His mind worked slowly, as though it had been affected by his illness. He could no longer read to himself. His advisers read him the things that they wanted him to know. He could not have known exactly what was going on. A newspaperman whom Vare formerly knew by his first name called on him in 1931 and was not recognized. When Vare called at the executive offices at Harrisburg, in 1931, he did not remember Attorney General William A. Schnader; and for a time he could not recall F. S. Stahlnecker, secretary to Governor Pinchot. And it was only after some moments that he recognized the man who had played so large a part in barring him from the senate, Governor Pinchot himself.

I last saw the leader in 1932. I called at his Atlantic City home with a letter of introduction from a close friend of Vare's, who was later a member of Mayor Moore's cabinet. This time I had difficulty in entering. Mrs. Vare had come to the door. I told her of my letter and asked her to give it to the Senator. She said, "He cannot see; come in and read it to him." I then saw the Senator stretched out at full length on a lounge, and he seemed all but unconscious. He gave me no word of greeting, and I began reading the letter. Before I had a chance to finish it, he wanted to know if my purpose was to write his life. I started to explain that I was writing a book on the Philadelphia organization and that he was part of it. He gruffly said, "I do not want any of it, then; my daughter is already doing that." (I think the biography of which he spoke appeared in the Philadelphia *Inquirer,* January, 1933; it was called "My Forty Years in Politics," by William Scott Vare.) I then tried to recall to him our former talks, but he seemed oblivious of all that was said.

Mrs. Vare wavered, but the Senator was adamant. When I

started leaving, she hastened to the side of the Senator and said, "He is leaving, Will." Vare grunted, "Goodbye." I answered, "Goodbye, Senator" and left, admiring his unshakable will.

Before I left, however, I had spoken to Mrs. Vare as she stood a few feet from the couch. That day, in City Hall, I had happened to mention my proposed visit to a veteran committee-man—one who lived in Senator Vare's own ward, the 26th, in Philadelphia. He had known the Vare family for thirty years, and he had asked to be remembered to Mrs. Vare. He counted her a real friend. I told Mrs. Vare I had just talked to Mr. Thomas Neville and that he wanted me to bring her his friendly greetings. Her face remained expressionless, and then she said, "Neville—I don't know him." She turned toward Vare and repeated the name a couple of times. To my surprise, he rather promptly said, "Neville—the fellow lives around the corner."

Except for this recognition of the name of the old party worker, Senator Vare appeared entirely passive. He was then almost exclusively in the hands of his friends.

Just as a Boss standing behind public officials had brought them (and the public) to grief, so did this synthetic leadership standing behind the Boss bring him and his party organization to irremediable defeat. Vare made an inexcusable mistake in slating the vulnerable Edward Merchant, secretary of the Board of Public Education, for the important place of city controller. Before the primary campaign was well under way, the organization apostate, Benjamin Golder, made such devastating charges against Merchant on the score of irregularities in the purchase of real estate for the Board of Public Education that the board was forced to appoint an investigating committee. The newspapers carried solid pages of the testimony for a number of weeks, and the crusading *Record* in particular published much invective in its editorial columns against Merchant. Though he finally won the nomination, after the primary the organization substituted a respectable attorney, Chester N. Farr, a man of high standing, in his place. Unfortunately for the organization, however, Farr was also a member of the Board of Public Education, and the trend of sentiment against the organization and the revealed carelessness and extravagances of the school board could not be stopped. Farr lost the election.

A second blunder was Vare's sponsorship of an exchange of important county offices between two old-time ward leaders— register of wills Billy Campbell and Coroner Fred Schwartz. They were both colorful men, but in 1933 the electorate was more interested in real ability than color. Furthermore, Campbell was just finishing his third four-year term in a most lucrative office, and this switching of him over to the Coroner's office, or the other lifelong placeholder to the register of wills office, awakened no enthusiasm except in the two men concerned, while it did anger and incense many organization followers who thought that someone else should have been given a chance. Thus this particular move, while sacrificing a certain amount of goodwill within the organization, did nothing to awaken confidence among the voters.

Vare's next mistake can best be explained by the deadening effect of his paralytic stroke, for in a tampering with the municipal court in a critical year, 1933, he did what no boss in possession of his normal faculties would have done—he attempted to replace several judges with men of unquestioned loyalty to himself. Even though one of the shrewdest politicians in Philadelphia was a judge, and even though several other judges were the real leaders of wards, in actuality if not in name, and even though still others were powerful vote getters, and the popular presiding judge of the Common Pleas Court, No. 1, Harry S. McDevitt, was later mentioned in the newspapers as a possible successor to Vare, and was a candidate for governor in 1934, Philadelphia still liked to think of the judiciary as apart from politics, and favored the retention of sitting jurists unless there was some particular reason why they shouldn't stay on the bench.

The 1933 election caused Vare's stock to strike bottom. Newspaper headlines announced "New Deal Ends Vare's Rule," "Republicans Lose Entire Party Slate," "Leaders Discuss Shelving of Vare,"; and the *Inquirer* boldly announced in a double-column front-page editorial that "Vare Should Get Out! Philadelphia Republicans Require New Leadership." The Pittsburgh *Evening Pub-*

lic Ledger editorially stated that decisive as the election verdict was, it "must be considered less as an endorsement of President Roosevelt than as a repudiation of the Vare leadership in this city."

This talk persisted, and yet the indomitable Vare, with a courage that never lessened, continued as leader and boss until June, 1934. Nor did he draw on a velvet glove in his last days for the sake of maintaining his hold. He had always been described by his familiars as a tough ringmaster, and he remained that until his death. Those politicians who wanted to see him overthrown had no one big enough to do the act. Vare inspired fear, and not altogether without cause. Some men Vare had made had found that a step away from him, even after he was stricken, was a step toward oblivion. The shrewdest and most daring of these men had learned by 1933 that it was not safe to strike a boss unless one killed him. In February, 1934, the members of the City Committee decided to create a War Board, or advisory committee, of twenty-one members to act as "leader" in place of Vare. It was said that this plan was agreeable to Vare, who understood, after the tragic defeat of 1933, that he was not physically able to provide the necessary leadership. However, he wanted this committee of twenty-one under his control and suggested that it rely on a sub-committee of seven members—the idea being that these seven men would be Vare 'yes' men. The War Board refused his suggestion, and so he hurried home from Florida and scrapped the War Board.

Preceding the spring primary of 1934, the hopeful candidates called at Vare's home in Atlantic City to get his support. He still had power in the eyes of realistic candidates. At this time, and contrary to his custom of deciding for himself, he yielded to the advice of some of his loyal ward leaders and declared himself for Attorney General William A. Schnader, the Mellon-Grundy choice, for governor. But, though Schnader won the nomination, the credit was in no way Vare's; and the more strictly Vare candidates for lesser offices were defeated. Although when the legislature met in a special session at Harrisburg a week after the election Vare's lieutenants delivered his orders, and they were obeyed, yet it was clear to everyone Vare's day was ending.

The final fight that was to culminate in Vare's overthrow inevitably followed the May primary of 1934. For this political contest again revealed Vare's weakness, and this was important to those of the fifty ward leaders who had to be convinced that Vare was through. Congressman Waldron had been approved by Vare, and by Vare only, for a second term in Congress. His congressional district comprised thirteen wards, all definitely organization-controlled wards. Vare's pronouncement was made, as usual, without consulting any of the leaders of these thirteen wards. It was particularly resented at this time. Jerome Louchheim, later leader in chief of the organization and then particularly powerful in one of the wards, quickly organized the others into an opposition in order to beat Vare's choice. Eleven of the thirteen ward leaders signed up to support Waldron's opponent. Vare attempted to use the big stick on the unruly eleven, but party and political sentiment were against him; he was powerless to destroy. He then made an effort to have Waldron withdraw. Waldron refused and was badly defeated. Vare's weakness was now apparent beyond question to every ward leader in the city.

Furthermore, Edwin R. Cox, president of the City Council, and one of the strongest of Vare's supporters, was a candidate in the primaries for nomination to the office of lieutenant governor. He asked for Vare's approval, and supposedly received it. But Vare actually and publicly repudiated Cox and supported Harry B. Scott. Cox, who was a man in his own right and a highly esteemed public official, then and there determined to have Vare counted out for all time. He combined with the leaders who were working for Vare's extermination, in a way which I shall presently describe.

As I have said, Vare accepted little outside advice. Even in his darkest hours following his stroke, he made his own decisions, or accepted advice chiefly from his daughter Beatrice, and, after she married his personal physician, Dr. Shaw, from her husband; and to a lesser extent, from his wife, Mrs. Vare. The influence of his family was so pronounced that the term "petticoat government" was often heard. That Vare was going to continue to arrogantly refuse to share his responsibility with others was again demonstrated in June. He had been elected a member of the Republican National Committee in June, 1933, but was unable to attend the June meeting in 1934.[83] As his proxy, he did not send Senator Reed, or any other person in public life, but instead he sent his son-in-law, Dr. Shaw. Even Vare's closest political allies resented the choice.

The 1934 primary provided the machinery as well as the steam for the successful revolt, and those who aspired to power took advantage of it. It might be well here to describe in some detail just what the machinery was in a battle of this sort. It was the body of contact men in politics. In Philadelphia they were called division leaders. There were two division leaders in each of the 1,283 divisions that composed the fifty wards of Philadelphia. They were the base of the party pyramid, standing between the voters below them, whose personal needs they often satisfied, and the ward leader above them, who was personally responsible to the leader of the organization. After these division leaders had been elected, they met in their respective wards and elected a member (the ward leader or his personal representative) to the City Commitee. Because of the ward leader's control over patronage he could often determine the outcome of division contests.[84] The newly elected City Committee then met to pass upon the credentials of its members, and to elect a chairman. This chairman had long been James M. Hazlett, recorder of deeds and personal ambassador of Vare. So long as his man was chairman, Vare was the boss; when his representative could be forced out, Vare's power would be gone.

As I have said, the primary provided the machinery for finishing Vare's rule; and those who aspired to power took advantage of their chance. Jerome H. Louchheim put up $65,000, and so did the anti-Vare factors on the City Committee. When this money was given out in the fifty wards, no equal-protection clause was observed. The money was used to elect ward committeemen opposed to Vare's leadership. For example, the powerful Councilman Harry Trainer, leader of the 3rd Ward and prominent member of the new combine, was plotting to take the scalp of Victor Hamilton, the Vare leader of the 7th. Therefore, the primary money was turned over to a Trainer lieutenant in the 7th, who distributed it among the committeemen willing to elect Trainer's choice to the City Committee. Most of the committeemen followed the cash. So when the ward committee of the 7th met, Trainer's man was in the saddle.

The same tactics were followed in the 30th Ward, where Vare's Negro lieutenant Asbury was defeated for re-election to the City Committee and a Negro sponsored by Trainer was elected in his place. In the 43rd Ward, Jimmie Clark, president of the County Commissioners, and a Vare loyalist, was defeated by Councilman Daly. Daly was opposed to Vare, and the money went to him. There were fights for ward committeemen in three other wards, and Vare supporters won two, while the opposing group was successful in the third.

In theory, the elected members to a ward committee were free to choose whom they would as the ward's representative on the City Committee. In reality these ward committeemen were jobholders, or they wanted to be, and they voted as "order men" —according to the instructions of the appointing power. (In the old days Vare would introduce his candidate to the Ward committee with the remark, "Here is your ward leader—elect him.") Prior to the election of members to the City Committee in this particular election, Arthur D. Brenner, receiver of taxes and loyal to Vare, threatened to fire any of the employees under him who failed to support Vare men for re-election to the City Committee. This led Edwin R. Cox, president of the City Council, to get the Finance Committee to report favorably on a long-pending ordinance to transfer supervision of 140 water-meter readers, inspectors, and clerks from the receiver of taxes to the Bureau of Water Department of Public Works. Brenner's hand was stayed; the four anti-Vare committeemen were elected.

However, the insiders thought that the straw that finally broke the camel's back, so far as Vare's supremacy was concerned, was Hazlett's failure to save the county commissioner, Clark, from defeat. (These two men were personal enemies, but both were steadfast Vare lieutenants.) Clark lost his fight for re-election by two votes; had Hazlett—who held the power over jobs—applied pressure, he might have saved Clark, and weakened the fight against his own seat as chairman of the City Committee.[85]

Thirty of the fifty city committeemen (ward leaders) were claimed for the insurgents by Judge Harry S. McDevitt on June 5, the day before the annual meeting of the City Committee. The series of defeats (indications of the leader's weakness) since Vare's stroke in 1928 had a cumulative force great enough to blot out fear of reprisals, and to change loyalties as houses long lived in are changed after a fire or a flood. The feeling of despair and resentment, too, was so expertly organized that when the committee met, even the faithful knew that the fight to save the Old Boss had at last failed. Sheriff Richard Weglein spoke for Senator Vare's friends when he asked Mr. Hazlett to withdraw as candidate for re-election as chairman of the Republican City Committee. Hazlett agreed, saying, "All you gentlemen know that after all, I put every personal ambition aside for party unity."

Councilman Trainer did not want the post and at a sercet caucus, attended by thirty-two ward leaders opposed to Vare, arranged for the election of Cox. Promptly after Hazlett withdrew Councilman Edward A. Kelly, newly elected committeeman from the 34th Ward and legal counsel for Vare in his fight before the United States Senate, placed Councilman Cox's name in nomination. He was elected unanimously.[86]

When Vare, who was convalescing at his Atlantic City home, heard about the collapse of his political power, he did not appear surprised. He merely remarked, "I have no comment." Two months later he died of a heart attack. He had never acknowledged defeat, and although his family were protesting at the "huge drain on their treasury for the upkeep of the party without compensating return," Vare himself was planning a comeback. After the new combine had gained control of the Republican City Committee, Vare never voiced a protest for public consumption. But he had not surrendered; for he had made comebacks before, and he thought he could do it again. So he was biding his time. Porch conferences had been resumed. Loyal Vare lieutenants were invited down to the shore once again. They began shopping around looking for tie-ups. The Vare men were but mildly interested in the coming November election, but were looking forward to the the mayoral and councilmanic fights the next year.

"Will I retire from politics?" Vare had repeated after a newspaperman who was interviewing him in 1931. "Listen," he answered, "does a duck retire from water?"[87] On the Sunday night before his death, he was discussing political plans for more than an hour with Sheriff Richard Weglein, who visited the veteran leader at his home in Berkeley Square. His unshakable courage was still unshaken. It was death that interrupted his plans.

About two weeks after Vare's defeat, a banquet was given to Edwin Cox, who in addition to being President of the City Council was also vice president of the Atlantic Refining Company. General William W. Atterbury, president of the Pennsylvania Railroad, was there, and congratulated Cox and his associates on the new leadership. Zimmerman of the U.G.I. (the gas utilities), bankers, and representatives of great economic interests also attended. As one recognized the personification of special privilege at the banquet table, one was reminded that Vare had defied Atterbury in the mayoralty campaign in 1931 and that it was a Vare stalwart, Senator Sam Salus, who had plainly told Elisha Lee, vice president of the Pennsylvania Railroad, to keep out of Philadelphia politics. But the big money is hard to keep down. The weakest ward leader knows that "dough is boss" and that even a ward leader is nothing but a straw man unless he has a bundle or is allied with someone who has. Metropolitan democracy has substituted not ballots for bullets, but dollars for bullets. Ballots only rarely and for brief stretches of time go against the political armies with the greatest war chests.

When Cox was made chairman of the City Committee, he bravely said that he would be chairman of the whole committee and "under no circumstances be dominated by any individual." This fine statement was about as reasonable to believe as the assertion that all voters are equally powerful in a democracy, or that one man's political influence is as great as another's. There were both giants (a few) and pygmies on the City Committee, and all history shows that the giants will bulk large in the forming of policies and the preparation of slates. In any great institution—

political, religious, commercial—there must be someone capable of saying yes and no. Cox was chairman, but Trainer, who was politically shrewd, wealthy, and could quote Shakespeare accurately (particularly *Richard III*), might have had the job in the spotlight had he desired it.

And then there was Charles Brown, president judge of the Municipal Court, a politician with a Cardinal Richelieu complex. Not only was he one of the most politically astute leaders in Philadelphia, but as president judge he controlled hundreds of desirable court positions. These jobs were a compelling whip, and even though a bar primary voted against him as it did in 1933, the electorate voted for him. His offices in City Hall were visited by strings of ward leaders coming and going. He heard each one privately and made a brief comment: "His advice is good."

Shortly after the change in leadership Brown appeared to be the liaison officer standing between the ward leaders (of whom he was one) and Louchheim and the utilities. He was, of course, a lawyer, though since boyhood he had had no preoccupation other than politics. He was fairly tall and slender, with a small head and alert, seeing eyes. He was just as much at home in the rough-and-tumble politics among the Negroes and whites of his ward as he was in making a brief address at a formal banquet at the Bellevue Stratford. He had served in the state legislature before Penrose made him a judge. One story can serve to illustrate his attitude quite as well as would a hundred. One of the judge's ward committeemen had been defeated some years before when he first tried to win election to the party committee. A month later he asked His Honor to put one of his constituents on probation for a year instead of sending him to jail. The judge quickly retorted, "You were beaten at the primary. Win your division, and then I'll talk to you." His biggest personal problem just now arose from the fact that he was on the bench. Philadelphians did not like to think of their judges in politics, and the newspapers were not kind to the judges who were. It was only in personal conversation with those who knew the facts that the importance of Judge Brown to the new leadership was made manifest. Jerome H. Louchheim, millionaire contractor, friend and ally of General

William W. Atterbury, was the financial angel of the new leadership. And in politics, as in the gentler field of music, he who pays the piper calls the tune. Louchheim was sixty years of age; his stock-breeding establishment in Maryland was said to be one of the finest in the world. He did not desire political office, he said, but he would give advice to the new political leaders should they ask for it.[88]

Edmund Burke told the electors of Bristol in 1780 that "my canvass of you was not on the 'change,' nor in the county meetings; it was at the customhouse; it was at the council; it was at the treasury; it was at the admiralty. I canvassed you through your affairs, and not your persons." And these electors rejected Burke.

Now Vare never made this mistake. He and his city-wide organization canvassed his constituents in Philadelphia through "their persons;" and for forty years, except for rare interruptions, the Vares received the support of their sovereign—the voters of America's most aristocratic city. What a politician does to capture the attention of his electorate cannot be evaluated until one learns of the electorate's response, the votes cast on election day. If the leader's appeals are those that win majorities or pluralities at the ballot box year after year, then one can mark that leader's conception of human nature in politics as realistic.

Some political leaders, like Theodore Roosevelt and Boies Penrose, are university men; and others, like Al Smith and W. S. Vare, are not. In either case, however, political leadership is not learned at college, nor is it denied to those who do not have the advantages of this more formal training. A political boss is a natural phenomenon and not a legal or academic creation. To describe him, one inevitably describes the environment that produced him. Vare was the prototype of these Philadelphians—the conservative, matter-of-fact, uneducated, hard-working majority who actually lived in the fifty wards of Philadelphia, the interminable city of small homes, block on block of duplicate houses, wall to wall, on narrow, treeless streets—and who preferred to live peacefully under a boss rather than fretfully under a reformer.

He never pretended to be a preceptor in ethics, a Savonarola
fighting social injustice, a crusader tilting at economic wrongs.
He was the champion of the existing order, and until the Great
Depression, his people were too.

His life was more like a Horatio Alger story than any that
Alger ever wrote (Alger, in failing to write about politicians,
neglected his richest materials in American life). From an obscure
beginning, through incessant toil, a flair for judging the drift of
public sentiment and the temper of men, a word unquestioned
in personal dealings, and an invincible spirit, he became more
than a millionaire; he became Boss of a great city.

Vare's passing as the political boss of Philadelphia was a
natural thing caused by the attrition of men and events over a
period of time. It was like the collapse of an old oak whose roots
had been loosened by wind and rain so that the tree could not
help falling before the next storm. The eclipse of the last, and
perhaps the greatest, of the Vares can more adequately be explained by this analogy than by saying that the Boss's overthrow
was sudden, like the toppling of a tree struck by lightning.

Vare's death was hailed by the press of the country as the
end of bossism in American cities. The Associated Press described
him as "one of the last of the old-time political bosses who 30
years ago controlled key cities of the nation. . . . Vare's passing
marked the end of a career identified with the colorful and tur-
bulent days when American politics were guided by a handful of
'strong men.' He was one of the last surviving bosses on the
political scene." The United Press declared that "Vare's death
brings to an end one of the most colorful political machines in the
country and one which caused Lincoln Steffens to call Philadelphia
'corrupt and content' back in the muckraking days of the early
20th century." The Philadelphia *Record* was the most optimistic
of all, for it believed that Vare's death marked "the ending of an
era—the era of one-man boss rule in American politics. Vare was
among the last in that fading army of political czars. . . . The
death of William S. Vare coincides with the passing of an epoch
in American politics."[89] It described Kelly, the head of the Democratic party in Philadelphia, as the "democratic leader who

symbolized the doom of gang rule in this city." The New York *Times* and the Philadelphia *Bulletin,* however, were more realistic. "It does not follow that Vareism will not appear again in Philadelphia. It is the conditions of great and sometimes of smaller cities that invite and create the boss," was the comment of the *Times*.[90] The *Bulletin* in commenting on Vare's death observed, "It is commonly said that the sort of politics which the Vare machine played and which has been so markedly identified with Tammany, has passed and that these old-time 'bosses' will have no successors in the New Deal. It is a worthy hope. But the appetite for spoils is a normal human endowment. The victor claims his reward. And the expansion of government has increased the number of plums in the administrative pudding to satisfy quivering palates and itching fingers. The opportunities for the Vares and Crokers, the Fitzgeralds and Curleys of Boston, are not less today than in the past—rather are more and greater. Only an alert, vigilant citizenry will prevent the setting up of a new 'Vare' dynasty in Philadelphia."[91]

It is significant that the domination of William Scott Vare was destroyed not by a revolution, a revolt of an awakened people whose political habits were undergoing a vast transformation, but by a *coup d'état* of palace intriguers. Philadelphia (and other American cities) will have a boss until the political duties imposed upon its citizens are reduced so much that these citizens can satisfy their political obligations unaided; or until Philadelphians become so educated that they will demand (and receive), as a right, from their official government, the security and service that the politician now gives as a favor. The boss bridges the gap in the Great Society between the unseen environment on one hand and the inadequate citizen on the other. So long as there is this gap, there will be a boss.[92]

FOOTNOTES

1. William S. Vare, *My Forty Years in Politics.*
2. Aug. 9, 1934.
3. Pittsburgh *Public Ledger*, Feb. 5, 1931.
4. *Ibid.*, Dec. 6, 1929.
5. Philadelphia *Record*, Aug. 8, 1934.
6. *Forty Years.*
7. Hearings, p. 505.
8. *Forty Years.*
9. *Ibid.*
10. *Ibid.*
11. *Ibid.*
12. Hearings, pp. 497, 548.
13. *Ibid.*
14. *Ibid.*, p. 548.
15. *Ibid.*
16. *Ibid.*, p. 494.
17. *Ibid.*, p. 537.
18. *Ibid.*, p. 563.
19. Hearings.
20. *Ibid.*, p. 539.
21. *Forty Years*, p. 155.
22. *Congressional Record*, 69: 310.
23. Hearings, p. 537.
24. *Ibid.*
25. *Ibid.*, p. 554.
26. *Ibid.*, p. 494.
27. *Ibid.*
28. *Congressional Record*, 69: 303.
29. Hearings, p. 494.
30. *Ibid.*, p. 494.
31. *Ibid.*
32. *Ibid.*, p. 495.
33. *Congressional Record*, 69: 303.
34. Hearings, p. 567.
35. *Ibid.*, p. 568.
36. *Ibid.*, p. 567.
37. *Ibid.*, p. 569.
38. *Ibid.*, p. 631.
39. *Congressional Record*, 69: 239.

40. *Forty Years,* p. 159.

41. *Congressional Record,* 69: 316.

42. Hearings, p. 607.

43. A New York *Times* editorial described the overlordship of the Vares thus: "In Philadelphia it was supreme, except when interrupted by a period of reform and the insurgencies of soreheads, who often returned to the fold. In Philadelphia the reign of the Vare de Vares was sometimes so perfect as to be comic, as when whole wards would scarcely cast a single Democratic vote. There were not Democrats enough to make a show. They had to be encouraged, protected. Almost it might be said that bounties had to be paid them." (Aug. 8, 1934.)

44. *Pittsburgh Public Ledger,* June 21, 1931.

45. Vare's devotion to his family and the family's devotion to him were incontestably a significant source of his strength. He was never alone. He once said that it was only a kind mother and a divine providence that had enabled him to do what he had done. As I have said, the brothers never acted without consulting each other. As one of their friends said, "W. S. and Edwin Vare, as brothers, completely lost all identity in each other. It was always 'we.' . . . There was never a question of a division of personalities, and about the greatest on earth to E. H. was 'our Bill,' and the greatest to W. S. was 'our Ed.'" As for his wife and children, in April, 1933, a friend of Vare's immediate family wrote to one of my friends: 'On many instances he [W. S.] would phone two or three times daily from Washington and would often ride three hours on the train to Philadelphia to spend an hour with her [his wife], and return on the next train to vote on a bill. In the heat of a political campaign, with meetings in all parts of the city, he would often rush home, like a boy, for a few minutes, say "I just wanted to see how you were," and dart out, perhaps, to another extremity of town. . . . If there was any little illness at home, it was not uncommon for him to phone three or four times a day." This personal statement may be lyrical, but there can be no doubt that family devotion greatly added to W. S.'s strength.

46. Cf. Philadelphia *Evening Bulletin,* July 7, 1931.

47. Aug. 8, 1934.

48. Philadelphia *Evening Bulletin,* "Men and Things" column, Aug. 9, 1934.

49. Pittsburgh *Public Ledger,* May 9, 1932.

50. Philadelphia *Record,* Aug. 1, 1931.

51. *Ibid.*

52. Philadelphia *Evening Bulletin,* July 30, 1931. Vare had real administrative ability, but much of it was wasted because he was

first the politician, the boss who must keep his power by keeping his henchmen satisfied. Weeding out the deadwood on the municipal payroll in order to cut government expenditures in Vare's mind did not mean getting rid of those who performed their governmental duties inefficiently; it meant getting rid of the men who were non-producers in their own divisions. A former precinct captain of Vare's in an open letter to the Pittsburgh *Public Ledger* in 1931 wrote: "When Bill Vare was made president of the Board of Mercantile Appraisers in 1900, he lost no time about revolutionizing the methods and policies of that body. The office of the board, prior to his incoming, had been a lounging-place for political hangers-on. It had the atmosphere of a ward club. Its methods were slip-shod and irresponsible. Vare promptly made it a business office, weeded out its idlers and gave it a definite administrative policy. He has always, at every stage of his career, been a stickler for efficient and courteous administration. When he became Recorder of Deeds he found that office richocheting along like a corner cigar store. Within three months he made it one of the most efficiently conducted offices in City Hall." (June 21, 1931.)

53. Senatorial Campaign Expenditures Investigation, p. 497.

54. Philadelphia *Record,* June 18, 1931.

55. Feb. 21, 1931.

56. Senatorial Campaign Expenditures Investigation, p. 505.

57. *Ibid.,* p. 504.

58. *Forty Years.*

59. In the 1926 senatorial primary.

60. Senatorial Campaign Expenditures Investigation, p. 575.

61. *Ibid.*

62. *Ibid.*

63. Aug. 9, 1934.

64. *Ibid.*

65. Philadelphia *Evening Bulletin.*

66. Pittsburgh *Public Ledger,* June 11, 1931.

67. Philadelphia *Record,* June 18, 1931.

68. The bonds were purchased over a long period of time beginning in 1907 and ending in 1929. Additional items in the estate include $416,993.24 in cash (one is reminded that at the time of Penrose's death more than a quarter of a million dollars in cash was found in his safety vault); 1,307 shares of the Vare Construction Company, listed at $191,645; 75 shares of the Jewish World Publishing Company, listed at no value; 41,475 shares of the Philadelphia Daily News, listed at $41,475; 49 shares of the Philadelphia Dispatch Publishing Company, listed at $49. There were a number of items of personal property—jewelry, furniture, etc.—which made up a large

list, but which were appraised at the approximate low total of $500. One can imagine what the figure might have been had this property been valued for bail rather than for inheritance-tax purposes. (Information secured April 29, 1935, through the courtesy of a prominent Philadelphia attorney.)

69. The Philadelphia *Record* described how the machinery of the Vare organization worked: "The setup of his machine was simple. His contracting concern got the fat contracts from the utilities and other corporations that found it advisable to keep in his good graces. The little fellows got jobs on the public payrolls. The contracts were usually lucrative. Most of them were on a cost-plus basis. The political jobs that went to the door-bell pullers were never scarce in the good old days. There was always room for another and especially for those who were on the opposite side of the political fence and had a real political or nuisance value. The depression put a serious crimp into Vare's open-handed distribution of political plums. Jobs were the life blood of the Vare organization. When they became hard to find, when henchmen were fired because of depleted city finances, the days of the organization were numbered. . . . The most important prize that will be at stake in the days that are to come will be the juicy contracts that went to the Vare Construction Company in return for political favors. Jerome H. Louchheim, millionaire contractor, who financed the revolt that overthrew the Vare leadership, is expected to make an effort to get any profitable contract that happens to be waiting for the taker." (Aug. 8, 1934.)

70. Pittsburgh *Public Ledger,* Dec. 6, 1929.

71. *Ibid.*

72. Hearings, p. 493.

73. Hearings, p. 682.

74. Hearings, p. 107.

75. Hearings, p. 575.

76. Hearings, p. 578.

77. Pittsburgh *Public Ledger,* Dec. 6, 1929.

78. Pp.135-36.

79. Philadelphia *Bulletin,* Feb. 5, 1932.

80. Philadelphia *Record,* June 18, 1931.

81. In the spring of 1935 the Bar Association of Philadelphia cited charges of professional misconduct against Senator Salus and seven other attorneys. These men were required to stand trial before the five president judges of the Common Pleas Court. On April 15 six of the attorneys (including Senator Salus) were ordered disbarred and two others were found not guilty of professional misconduct but were censured by the court. Those familiar with the situation were not surprised at the evidence produced in court, but

there was speculation over why certain other attorneys were not cited for trial along with these eight. A letter to me dated February 18, 1935, from an independent Republican of unquestioned integrity and intelligence is in point:

"Sam Salus was getting too big. A little over a month ago a testimonial banquet was given him at the Bellevue at which there were about 1,000 persons present, including then Governor Pinchot and state senators from throughout the state. He was made much of and there was talk of his taking over the leadership of the Republican Party. He was undoubtedly a potent factor. . . .

"In any event, there was plenty of reason for pulling the Saluses down and the Bar Committee offered the opportunity. The wise ones will point out also that the Chairman is a Louchheim man and that Salus and Louchheim have been leading opposing factions for some years past."

82. Feb. 24, 1932.

83. Ironically enough, Vare was elected to the highest peak in Pennsylvania Republicanism by the state committee and allowed to wear the toga that had once graced the shoulders of Cameron, Quay, and Penrose only after the political power that had brought him this privilege was crumbling, only after he was too feeble to exercise it. And in the minds of some observers, it led indirectly to his defeat in 1933, for, lulled into a false sense of security by this new honor, he made the fatal mistake of attempting to hand-pick the row office slate in the city election.—*Ledger,* Aug. 12, 1933.

84. The vital importance of jobs to a party organization should be noted, for they are not only the backbone of the organization but the heart that keeps it going. That their significance was clearly understood by David H. Lane, "the Peerless Leader," was most natural (but that we should have his best thought on this matter explicitly reported in a newspaper was decidedly unnatural). In the heat of the 1901 campaign in Philadelphia he told the committeemen of the 19th Ward the stuff of his thinking on this key subject. His masterly statement was reported in the *Public Ledger* of October 7 of that year, as follows:

"The cohesive power of the organization is offices. We have 10,000 office-holders, and they are all ours. Under the present administration no man can get an office unless he is loyal to the organization. Only today the organization voted $40,000 for tax receipts. How could we do that if we didn't have the office-holders? If you want office or preferment in political life you will have to get it through the organization. The office-holders are the backbone of the organization. We have all of the office-holders and we want to keep them. Poles, Hungarians, Italians, and other foreigners, when they come here vote the Republican ticket. Why? Because we have the offices, and they expect favors from office-holders.

"In New York they vote for Tammany for the same reason. Our organization bears the same relation that Tammany does to New York. If we would keep these voters we must retain control of the offices. Foreigners know that they cannot get favors except through our organization. It is especially important that we should elect the District Attorney, not because Mr. Weaver is a candidate but because there is great power in that office, and it is to the advantage of the organization to have a friend in it."

Later this same leader said: "The ownership of the offices means the power for distributing patronage and for conferring favors upon citizens generally, who in return, will support the organization. It is through this far-reaching power that the great Republican party is given its majority in this city and state. Without the offices this great organization would crumble and fall." And a member of Mayor Moore's cabinet, an old and seasoned ward leader, put the same proposition into his own words in 1932. "Jobs, of course, is the basis of it all. That is absolutely the basis of it. Where would the organization be without places?" I need not add that this question of patronage was particularly urgent to the Republicans in 1935, for the Democrats had captured some important posts and had an even chance of winning more. It followed that the future of the Republican party depended in large measure on its ability to obtain jobs for its workers.

85. Much of the detailed undercover work in throwing over Vare was done by ward leader XYZ, leader of the XYZ ward, and one of the city's twenty-two councilmen. He opposed Vare in 1933 by campaigning for the lucrative register of wills post. He based his campaign plea on "No More Vare." He polled 48,900 votes, spent $15,000 and was defeated. He said that Vare had made a mistake in "letting him go away mad." "I spent $15,000 in the primary, and Vare never said a word about making it up. Vare was too damn tight. He fought Earle, Penrose's candidate for mayor, in 1911. When Earle was nominated, Penrose called for Bill Vare and said, 'How much did you spend?' Vare thought that he had spent about $250,000. 'All right,' said the Senator, 'I will give you my check.' Bill Vare never did this to me. I worked with Brownie [Judge Charles Brown]. Louchheim put up the money. I rounded up a majority of the City Committee. One day Eddie Cox asked if I had been hearing anything. I said that I had. When I told him that we already had a majority for the new leadership, he agreed to serve as chairman. He was sore because Vare had not supported him for the lieutenant governor in the primaries." (Interview at the home of XYZ, Aug. 30, 1934.)

86. This group who seized control of the City Committee also unhorsed Miss Marion Pyle, who had given a lifetime of service to the Vares and who had been in control of the women's organization.

87. Philadelphia *Inquirer,* July 30, 1931.

88. Even during the days following Vare's defeat there were some unreconstructed Vare leaders who remained outside the fold or who had to be shown before they unequivocally accepted the Louchheim-Brown-Cox-Trainer leadership. Senator Sam Salus was one of the most powerful and resourceful of these, and his influence was increasing until he was disbarred for professional misconduct. Sheriff Richard Weglein was probably the one most capable of providing leadership for the scattered Vare leaders who had not become committed to the new regime. Councilman Clarence Crossan and Recorder of Deeds James Hazlett were in this coterie. In May, 1935, there were a number of leaders, but there was no towering Penrose or Vare among them who could charge the imagination of either the voters or the ward leaders. The Republicans in Philadelphia were not accustomed to party defeat and their morale was low. They were casting about and hoping that mistakes made by the Democrats, and their resulting unpopularity, would bring about a revulsion of feeling in favor of the Republicans. The man or the group that named the next mayor would be a power, but who this would be could not be known at that time, and, besides, the Democrats might win. Furthermore, Louchheim was more the financier and less the politician type. He helped finance the anti-Vare revolt, but unless Philadelphia obtained money from the federal government to spend on contracts there was no point, as one leader remarked, "in Louchheim putting up money to control an administration that would have no money to spend." Both in the nation and in the city of Penn and Vare the Republicans lacked leadership and morale. There was often conflict rather than cooperation; there was an unwillingness or an inability to act in accord with the new times.

89. Aug. 8, 1934.

90. *Ibid.*

91. *Ibid.*

92. And of course it is incontestably true that the price of good government is not only an alert citizenry but also an organized citizenry—a citizenry organized right down into the wards and division even as the professional politicians organize. For as Burke once said, "if bad men combine, good men must associate," or to quote a modern authority:

"This opens the question to be considered, the cause of political parties. People often discuss whether they are a good or an evil. In fact they are both; for they are groups, and exhibit the tendencies for good and evil that all groups possess to a greater or less extent. The essential point for our immediate purpose is that under normal conditions they are as inevitable as the tides in the ocean. Small bodies of water have no tides, but in large ones tides exist whether we want them or not; and in like manner the existence of parties is greatly affected by the size of the political community, that is by the number of people called upon to form a collective opinion on questions of policy or candidates for public office. . . .

"The reason why the necessity for political party increases with the size of the community is to be found in the fact that the larger the number of minds the greater difficulty of procuring an agreement among them, or a majority of them."—A. L. Lowell, *Public Opinion in War and Peace,* chap. 4.